How to Publish Your Own Book

By

BERNARD NEARY

LENHAR PUBLICATIONS, DUBLIN

Foreword

by Gabriel Rosenstock

A *oibhinn a leabhráin do thriall......* Self-publishing must not be confused with vanity publishing. Self-publishing has a noble tradition whereas, in the main, vanity publishing does not. Do not be deceived by advertisements - even in quality newspapers - which suggest that a certain publishing house, which shall be nameless, is eagerly awaiting to publish your manuscript, or that an agent in Hollywood is on the hot line, waiting anxiously for news of the Big One.

Publishers and literary agents are up to their oxters in unsolicited manuscripts. If you have had no luck with publishers and agents you may well decide that the time is ripe to self-publish. If the manuscript is a year old, give it a final dusting, blow away the chaff and give it a lash!

Bernard Neary has provided us with a lively guide to the art of self-publishing; it is a spirited gallop along uneven terrain but we follow him readily, knowing that he has been down that road before. Many readers will be grateful to him and if you benefit from his selfless advice, don't forget to invite him to your first launch and to thank him for marking the playing field.

Publishers are not infallible. They miss the odd good title from time to time or stipulate changes that may not be fully acceptable to you. Self-publishing, ideally, should be a last resort, so have a go if all else fails. Bernard Neary makes it look rather simple, really. O sancta simplicitas! When you've finished reading this book, read it again; extract the main points and keep a ledger. Tick off the things to do, keep details of dates, money coming in and going out. Go n-éirí go geal leat!

Gabriel Rosenstock

Dedication

This book is dedicated to the suffering people of East Timor, the former Portuguese colony invaded by the brutal military might of Indonesia in 1975. Following a violent campaign of genocide in which nearly one third of the native peoples (population now approximately 650,000) were brutally massacred or starved to death by the Indonesian terror machine, East Timor was annexed by the invaders as its 27th province. Several United Nations Resolutions condemning the invasion were passed in 1976.

That the invasion was brutal is in no doubt - an entire Australian film crew was tortured and murdered by the invaders. That repression and terror continue is in no doubt - hundreds of students were massacred during a peaceful protest to the cemetery in Dili, the capital of East Timor, in 1992. That you as an individual can do something is in no doubt - the components of the American Dream, Nike, LA Gear and Adidas consumer products, are manufactured in Javan towns - check the label on your purchases and if it is "Made in Indonesia", boycott it!

If you are concerned about the unfortunate people of East Timor, people who like ourselves in the 1700's and 1800's had no friend or voice in the world, you can join the East Timor Society, 210 Le Fanu Road, Ballyfermot, Dublin 10 Phone (01) 623 3148. For a full appraisal on this unfortunate nation's suffering, you can read "Indonesia's Forgotten War: the Hidden History of East Timor" by John Taylor (Zed Books, London 1991).

Other Titles from Lenhar Publications (*out of print):

"A History of Cabra and Phibsborough"*

"North of the Liffey - A Character Sketchbook"*

"Lugs - The Life and Times of Jim Branigan"*

"Irish Lives - The Irish in Western Australia"

"Confessions of a Court Clerk"

"Waiting for the 22"

"Dublin 7"   (All titles by Bernard Neary).

"Rose of Cabra" by Rose O Driscoll

"Seoda Oga" by the Schoolchildren of Scoil Oilibhéir, Blanchardstown, Dublin 15.

Introduction

By Councillor Paddy Farry

It is with great personal satisfaction that I associate myself with Bernard Neary's efforts relating to self-publishing. As a long-time supporter of Community-based arts, I welcome the publication of his book, which I feel will have a tremendous impact on the whole area of Community arts throughout the island of Ireland. As "How to Publish Your Own Book" offers advice and useful hints on all aspects of publishing, the information given by Bernard Neary can be adapted to other areas besides print, like publishing audio cassettes or compact discs.

Recent trends in the book industry has seen a significant growth in the area of self-publishing. As our society has developed and become more advanced, people are becoming more self-confidant. If someone has written a story - be it a novel, a true confession or a compilation of poetry - they do not now see a rejection by the established publishing world as the end of the road. A more confidant society is now looking to the area of doing it themselves, and Bernard Neary has mapped out the course of self-publishing for any energetic writer, in a clear, step-by-step, easy to follow manner.

In my support for Community arts over the years, I have been associated with many projects, including book publishing. I had the honour of being instrumental in the publishing of a book of poetry by an 85-year-old constituent of mine, Rose O Driscoll, entitled "Rose of Cabra". I knew Rose well from my involvement in local politics in the Dublin 7 area, and the association with her writing talents gave me a deep insight into the whole area of self-publishing and the benefits that it can bring not only to individuals and communities but to local economies as well.

Bernard Neary's book is timely, coming as it does hot on the heels of the success of an English self-published author, Jill Paton Walsh, whose novel "Knowledge of Angels" was short-listed for the 1994 Booker Prize. I welcome it for the assistance and benefits it can bring to the area of Community arts and am delighted to be associated with it through this introduction.

If anyone is contemplating writing their own book, the process is now laid out in a simple fashion. If you have been unsuccessful in securing a publisher for your work, be it a novel, book of poetry, music cassette or comic strip, take heart, take the plunge and good luck to you.

Councillor Paddy Farry, Dublin, Christmas 1994

Acknowledgements

I wish to thank the following for their assistance and help to me while carrying out this project: Gabriel Rosenstock for his advice, help and great enthusiasm; Peter Donnelly for his excellent sketches; Seosamh Mac Ionmhain, as an cheartúcháin go léir a rinne sé i gCaibidil 10; Dónall Ó Luanaigh, Keeper (Collections), National Library of Ireland, for his helpful comments; Peter Sirr of the Irish Writers Centre for the facilities made available to me and Geraldine Keogh for all the time spent proof reading. Finally, I would like to say a special word of thanks to my local Public Representative, Councillor Paddy Farry, for his kind help, assistance and enthusiasm.

Copyright (c) 1994 Bernard Neary.
Illustrations (c) 1994 Peter Donnelly, Phone (01) 864 0004.

Published by Lenhar Publications, 7 Croaghpatrick Road, Dublin 7 Phone (01) 838 7283. Typesetting and origination by Typeform Limited, Newtown Industrial Estate, Clonshaugh, Dublin 17 Phone (01) 847 5822. Printed by Futureprint Limited, 103 Grangeway, Baldoyle Industrial Estate, Dublin 13 Phone (01) 839 2070. Distributed by Easons Limited, Brickfield Drive, Dublin 12 Phone (01) 4536211 and Boucher Road, Belfast, Northern Ireland Phone (0232) 381200.

Paper supplied by Mc Naughton Paper Ireland Limited, 67 Cherry Orchard Industrial Estate, Dublin 20 Phone (01) 626 1601 and 8 Duncrue Road, Belfast BT3 9BH Phone (0232) 774004.

A very special thanks to AIB Smithfield, and Mr Jim Orange, Solicitor, without whose assistance this publication would not have been possible.

The Illustrationist: Peter Donnelly was born in Dublin in 1967 and grew up on the northside suburb of Finglas. Peter is a published illustrator and presently works in the animation industry.

Launched in the Irish Writers' Centre, 19, Parnell Square North, Dublin 1, and in the Old Museum Arts Centre, College Square North, Belfast, Winter 1994/5.

ISBN 0 9514707 7 9

Contents

Page

CHAPTER 1   Completing Your Manuscript 1

CHAPTER 2   Getting Sponsorship/Book Pricing 7

CHAPTER 3   Critical Comments 13

CHAPTER 4   ISBN 15

CHAPTER 5 Copyright 17

CHAPTER 6   Typesetting and Printing 21

CHAPTER 7   The Launch 29

CHAPTER 8   Distribution 35

CHAPTER 9   Getting the Publicity 43

CAIBIDIL 10   An Leabhar Gaeilge É? 57

CHAPTER 11   One Year Later 61

CHAPTER 12   And Finally. 65

What do you need from a Trade Printer and Binder?

- you need printing from mono to full colour on our Heidelberg presses up to B1
- you need folding on our H+H folders up to B1
- you need sewn blocks or books on our Müller Martini automatic thread-sewers
- you need to gather, stitch and trim on our Müller Martini Minute Man (6 stations and cover feeder)
- YOU NEED PERFECT BINDING ON OUR 24 STATION MÜLLER MARTINI NORMBINDER.

you also need   people who have the skills,
                people with the right attitude to quality,
                people with the right attitude to delivery-on-time

and who know that <u>YOUR JOB</u> is very important!

FOR QUOTATION **839 2070**
Janette Ashmore • Patrick Whelan • Caroline Kelly

FUTURE PRINT LIMITED
Grange Way, Baldoyle Industrial Estate, Dublin 13.
Telephone: 01-839 2070 • Fax: 01-839 2591

CHAPTER 1

Completing Your Manuscript

A sincere welcome to the world of self-publishing. As you come on board this journey through the unknown world of publishing, please remember that what you are reading is not a guide on how to write your own book but a guide on how to publish your own book - so there are no hints on how to write a novel or a local history!

After over ten years experience of publishing my own work both in Ireland and Western Australia, I feel that the time has come to inform the average punter that there is really no magical aura surrounding the publishing of a book. Nor is it a quagmire, in which the inexperienced will be swallowed up. Rather, it is a simple, step-by-step process that requires just a good knowledge of the book trade and how it works coupled with some persistence and hard slogging.

Rejected

You have laboured over your manuscript, be it a selection of poems, a novel, biography, childrens' story, collected short stories or a local history. If you were like me, you probably carried it around everywhere with you when you were working on it. Like a parent and new-born baby, you could never leave it on its own. Now your manuscript is nearing completion and you want to have it published. You have probably tried a number of publishers and basically drew a blank - you either filled a litter bin with rejection slips or were told any combination of the following: "Come back next year", "There are a number of books presently out on that topic, bring it back in two years", "The market is saturated with the subject". (If you have not tried many publishers, try "The CLÉ Directory of the Irish Book World", the "Writers' and Artists Yearbook",

CHAPTER 1: *Completing Your Manuscript*

"Books Ireland" and the weekly UK book trade magazine "The Bookseller" for possible publishers in your chosen subject).

I tried a number of publishers with my first book, "A History of Cabra and Phibsborough", and each one rejected it, all stating that it was purely of local interest. In desperation I asked two rejecting publishers could I put the book out myself and was told "no - sure you need to be a registered publisher and it would cost you £500 for an ISBN number"...."a bar-code will cost you £100". However, I was fortunate to know Dermot Bolger, the well-known poet, who kindly and professionally led me through the mysterious world of publishing. I dispensed with ISBN numbers for my first few books - imagine my surprise some years later when I discovered that the service is free and that a bar-code would not cost you a penny!

Of course, no publisher is going to advise you to go ahead and self-publish the work which they are rejecting - they know that you would be competing with them for shelf-space in the bookshops, even though your book might only be a humble local history! So if you have met with no success yet burning with desire and ambition to see your work in print, there is one choice that is clearly facing you: publish the book yourself!

Jill Paton Walsh had her novel rejected by so many publishers in the UK, both large and small, that she ended up bringing it out under her own Green Bay imprint. The novel, "Knowledge of Angels", was short-listed for the 1994 Booker Prize. So self-publishing is a realistic choice, for it is relatively easy to go down the road of self-publishing and I will now take you on a step-by-step process that will enable you to publish your work and market it.

Resource

It is worthwhile mentioning here that you have one resource that no publisher, large or small, has - the commitment and generous backing of all your friends, co-workers, family and life-partner. All those close to you will be delighted for you and will assist in your venture in whatever way that they can. This resource is an invaluable one and do not be afraid to take any help from whatever quarter offered.

Corporate Body

You don't have to be an individual to find it difficult to get a publisher to take on your book and the advice given here can also assist a company, organisation, trade union, tourist association, parish church, village community or even a

Government Department. For example, if you are the Governor of Mountjoy Prison you may wish, in the year 2000, to put out a book commemorating 150 years of the institution's history; a company may wish to publish an annual report and a village community or parish group may wish to put out a book on a local landmark, historical event or famous daughter or son of the neighbourhood. A Government Department may wish to publish an information booklet aimed at the general public or the Ulster Museum may wish to put out a book on Spanish Armada treasures. The following advice should enable any group to enter the exciting world of self-publishing.

Foreword

A good foreword by a suitable personality is a must for your book. You will probably have your own ideas, contacts and favourites in this regard, so I will not advise you. Fr FX Martin, the eminent historian, wrote a foreword to "Dublin 7" for me in 1992; Dermot Bolger wrote the foreword for a book of poetry by Rose O Driscoll entitled "Rose of Cabra" which I published in 1992. Other people who wrote forewords to books I published included Michael Keating TD, Charlie Haughey, Don Conroy and Brian Burke, former Premier of Western Australia. In all cases the foreword was personal to the published work and actually proved to be a most interesting feature of each particular title.

In any event, your non-fiction book will not be complete without a suitable foreword. From my own experience I have never encountered any difficulty and have found people to be most approachable and helpful in this regard. I have found that a simple letter setting out the content of the particular book, together with a draft, has secured agreement from a chosen individual to write a foreword. Novels, short stories and poems generally do not have a foreword, but you can break the rules - once you know them!

Acknowledgements

It is a good idea to have a page for acknowledgements, where you can set out all your sources, thus satisfying copyright requirements. You can also use this page to thank all those who assisted you in the project, including your proof-readers, sponsors and staff in libraries, newspapers, companies and institutions who may have been of assistance to you while creating the book, and family and friends who may have helped you along the way. People like to be thanked in this small way and it is nice to be appreciative. Most important of all, you put the names and telephone numbers of your typesetter, printer and distributor on this page.

CHAPTER 1: *Completing Your Manuscript*

If you have not got a distributor, put your own name, address and telephone number down here so that shops or individuals will know who or where to contact to get a copy of your book.

Proof Reading

You may, like me on my first three books, not know any typist and are unable to type. If so, do not worry. Bring your hand-written manuscript, duly proof-read, to your typesetter. Of course, you will have to pay for it to be typed, but it should not be prohibitively expensive. When typed, get proofs from the typesetter for final proof-reading and correction, if necessary. You are than ready for printing.

If your manuscript is typed you should ensure that it is pruned of all typing errors and refrain from an over-liberal use of commas, especially used in conjunction with conjunctions! You can get some friends or work colleagues to perform your proof-reading. It is a good idea to photostat three copies of your draft manuscript - either typed or handwritten - and get three people to proof-read, just in case one takes ill, loses the manuscript or forgets all about it. After all corrections have been made and when, and only when, you are ready to proceed to the publishing stage, bring your manuscript, on a computer disc or in type-written form, to the typesetter/printer.

It is worthwhile remembering that presenting your manuscript on computer disc will save quite a lot of money, as a manuscript, unless in perfect condition and of a readable form of print, would have to be retyped by the typesetter. If your manuscript is of a superior quality, that is if you had access to Desktop Publishing and your material is "camera-ready" (ready for printing), then lucky you - bring it directly to the printer, which will save you considerable typesetting costs. If this is the case, I would advise you to enlist the services of a typesetter or artist for your cover-design.

If your resources allow and if you know of a professional editor to cast an eye on the final proofs, all the better. Gremlins can appear out of nowhere. In addition, the trained editor can spot inconsistencies or worse still, an item that could lead to litigation. Consider this aspect seriously, as if your book contains libel, it will not be handled by a distributor and large bookshops; it might not be handled by local bookshops either.

CHAPTER 1: *Completing Your Manuscript*

Irish Writers Centre

The Irish Writers' Centre, 19 Parnell Square, Dublin 1, Phone (01) 872 1302, has information on publishing as well as reference books which would help you through the ins and outs of the industry. You can drop into the Centre and access their library, publications and information and avail of their photocopying facilities. The Centre also runs a variety of creative workshops. The Director of the Centre is Peter Sirr and you can write to him for details of their workshops and courses. It is an excellent back-up for today's writer and anyone coming in off the street is assured of some helpful assistance and back-up.

Another valuable back-up for anyone contemplating publishing their own work is their own local Arts Centre. Many Arts Centres run seminars and workshops on all aspects of writing - for example the Verbal Arts Centre, Cathedral School Building, London Street, Derry, Phone (0504) 266946, ran a workshop in October of this year on the production of comics and graphic novels; the cost was just £5 (concessions £2.50), underlining the accessibility of your local Arts Centre.

Viatores Christi?

Viatores Christi means travellers for Christ.
We are a lay missionary association, founded in
Ireland in 1960, which recruits and helps prepare people for
service in areas of need overseas.

What to we do?

Acknowledgeing the wealth of our life skills as well as our professional and work-related training we go to share our lives for a specific period of time.

We play an active part in the local Christian community through joining with others in various forms of service and through a friendly presence. We share and pass on our skills hoping to make ourselves dispensable.

Where do Viatores work?

Viatores Christi responds to requests for service
from any part of the world, provided the work
involved is seen to be genuinely worthwhile and
answers the needs as expressed by the community
and that there are suitable personnel available. Most
members are working in the Developing Countries of Africa,
Asia, and Latin America, but there are usually some involved
in areas of need in Europe, Canada and the U.S.A.

Like to know more

Viatores Christi

Travellers for Christ
38/29 Upper Gardiner Street, Dublin 1.
Phone 8749346/8728027 Fax 8749346

CHAPTER 2

Getting Sponsorship and Book Pricing

Holding down a PAYE job and your Prize Bond number not coming up means that you probably won't have the resources to fund the full cost of publication of your book. I had to sell my car in order to fund the publication of my first book, "A History of Cabra and Phibsborough". You will also have to keep in mind the fact that as a new published author, you will have to push very hard to sell both your book and yourself. The last thing you will have to remember is the fact that your printer may only give you thirty or sixty days credit, depending on what you both agree. Bearing this in mind, you will need to secure some sponsorship, as this will eliminate extremes of effort, like selling your car, in order to see your work in print.

The first thing you must realise when you are seeking sponsorship is you have got to have something to offer a prospective sponsor. It is pointless looking for support and giving your generous sponsors a mention in small print, in the acknowledgements section. There has to be a lot more give on your part in this regard.

Irish businesses can be extremely generous towards the arts, especially towards a good project. They will, of course, want to gauge your commitment to your project and will ask what benefits will accrue to them from their association. Here you will have to let them know your plan of action, the substance of your book, the target market, the likely response of newspapers and the localities/sectors in which you hope to make your greatest volume of sales. They will also need to know the print run.

Be Honest

There is a great need here for you to be entirely honest. You cannot tell a sponsor that your book will have an initial print run of 20,000 if you are only getting 2,000 copies printed. A sponsor can find out how many copies you are printing - and can also see through you if you are less than honest. Remember, your sponsor

CHAPTER 2: *Getting Sponsorship and Book Pricing*

is in business and has the experience and intuition to feel for a project - lie about it and you will be shown the door!

When I talk about sponsorship, I am not talking about big punts; what I am talking about is sponsorship in the region of £50 to £100 per company/organisation. In this day and age, with so many demands on business budgets, it is all that one can expect. If you even get £50 in some cases you will be doing very well but overall you should average £50 with little difficulty.

You may be able to highlight a particular firm in your book, for example, if it is a local history, you might research the history of some firms to incorporate them into the book. As a quid-pro-quo for researching and documenting a company's history, they may be willing to assist in the form of sponsorship. If it is a book on sport, you could mention the factory/office where a prominent amateur sportsperson is employed and if you are putting that sportsperson's photograph in the book, take it to show their place of employment. That should interest the company as a sponsor.

Draw up a list of prospective sponsors, then look at all the angles on how you can give each company value for money in the event of their supporting your work. You will find at the end of the day that companies and business people will be very approachable and only too willing to assist if both their interests and yours merge. You may come across a business person who is fond of the arts and who may wish to be associated with your work. Why not include them in the book in some way, for example, if it is a local history and are covering the building, you could include the business person in a photograph of the building; alternatively you could let them write the foreword. If you already have committed yourself on a foreword, they could write an introduction. Be flexible if you need the shillings!

I have incorporated both a foreword and an introduction in this book as an example of how it can be done.

Finally, I have said that you must give value for money in the area of sponsorship. Therefore, the number of sponsors should be limited, say to a maximum of ten or twelve, depending on your book. If you get a hundred sponsors, there is no way that they will get value for money - but the purchaser of your book will see your ten or twelve sponsors and this will guarantee some return for the support given. In any event a prospective sponsor will ask how many other sponsors will be included in the book and if it is felt that you have "gone over the top" in this regard, they will not support you. Again, you will have to be honest in this area; you cannot say that you will have only six sponsors when in fact you have fifty-six;

CHAPTER 2: *Getting Sponsorship and Book Pricing*

you will never be sponsored again. So consider the sponsorship market, set your target (ten or twelve) and go for it. When you have reached your target, leave it at that.

Don't forget to include your sponsors in your invitation list to the book launch - they have helped make your project the reality it has become. It is also a way of giving them value for money, as well as showing your deep gratitude for their genuine support. In any event they will be talking about *your* book and at the end of the day one of the best selling points for any book is word of mouth! They may even order a few dozen copies from you at cost price.

Arts Council

I have concentrated a lot on corporate sponsorship because I have never availed of any State grants scheme. You may satisfy the criteria for a Government grant in order to facilitate your work and if you are a published creative writer - or will be - you might like to apply to the Arts Council, 70 Merrion Square, Dublin 2, Phone (01) 661 1840 for a Bursary. The Arts Council of Northern Ireland, 181A Stranmillis Road, Belfast, Phone (0232) 381591 provide grants to writers resident in Northern Ireland. Under the Arts Council of Northern Ireland Awards grants are available for poetry, novels and short stories; local history may also be eligible for grant funding. The grants are awarded annually, every March, and the Awards Scheme is advertised in all major newspapers circulating throughout Ireland. Arts Council grants are a valuable source of assistance to the creative writer.

There may be sources of funding other than Arts Council grants, for example the Department of Education NI, Rathgael House, Balloo Road, Bangor, Co Down, Phone (0247) 270077 or Bord na Gaeilge, 7, Cearnóg Muirfean, Baile Átha Cliath 2, Guthán (01) 676 3222. CAFE - Creative Activity for Everyone, 23/25 Moss Street, Dublin 2, Phone (01) 677 0330, publish an excellent handbook which deals with all types of available funding in the Republic of Ireland and in Northern Ireland. Entitled "The Funding Handbook", it is an

CHAPTER 2: *Getting Sponsorship and Book Pricing*

excellent reference source. Your local Arts Centre may have a copy which you can refer to.

Pricing your Book

One of the most important aspects of publishing your own book is fixing a suitable price. You will have an idea what you would need to charge, so you will now have to gauge the market price necessary. To do this, just go to a big bookshop and have a look at all the books in the range of your particular manuscript, be it poetry, local history, biography, autobiography, novel or sport. Have a good look at similar publications and gauge the price you need to charge. Two rules of thumb - don't overprice and don't underprice. If you have a book of poetry that will run to fifty pages or so, a price of between £2.95 to £3.95 would be sustainable. A local history running to 100 to 140 pages would sustain a price of between £4.95 and £6.95. However, you would need to look at similar books and decide yourself what price would be suitable.

Your price would of course have to give sufficient return in order for you to cover your costs. However, if you do your sums and find that your book is still on the dear side, see how you can either trim costs or secure more sponsorship. You don't need to know your final price until the cover is printed, but you do need a price on the book if you want the big bookshops to take it.

When doing your sums, remember the charge or commission in the book trade: *fifty per cent* (50%) for a distributor and *thirty three to thirty five per cent* (33% to 35%) for a bookshop, based on the *retail* price of the book. If it is a very local publication, you may be able to get local outlets to accept a charge of 20% to 25%, but overall you are looking at a flat rate of 33%. So if your book retails at £3, you will get £2 for each book sold if supplying directly to bookshops yourself and £1.50 if supplying through a distributor. From the balance, either £1.50 or £2, you have to meet all your expenses, printing, typesetting, cover design, illustrations and launch.

You will have your estimate from both the printer and typesetter (alternatively, the printer may undertake the typesetting as well as the printing), and photographer and illustrationist, if applicable. Allow a maximum of £100 launch costs, to include the cost of invitation cards, and you now have a cost on the complete outlay. Say your total costs come to £4,500; if your print run is based on your estimate of 2,000 copies being sold through a distributor and if you have secured £500 in sponsorship, you will need to charge £4 per book in order to break even on sales of 2,000. However, it is crucial that you remember that from such a print run you just will <u>not</u> have 2,000 copies to sell, as complimentary

10

CHAPTER 2: *Getting Sponsorship and Book Pricing*

copies for reviews, newspaper and radio coverage, sponsors and people who helped you will come to about 300 copies. So assume having 1,700 copies available for sale.

Now, having carried out some preliminary market research, you feel that you can easily sell over 1,000 copies, you could assume sales of 1,500 copies. (If you sold the full 1,700 - remember those 300 complementary copies - you would be doing really well). Therefore, assuming 1,500 copies being sold you will have to charge £5.45 per copy to make a return on such anticipated sales. If your estimate works out around the even pound mark, charge 5p less - the 95p is a good figure, and it is best to charge £2.95, £3.95 etc. rather than the round sum in pounds).

Éigse Éireann

In the case of poetry an attractive volume can appear in a limited edition of 1 to 300, all individually numbered and signed. It is reasonable to charge £5 for such a volume but do check that your printer can specialise in such a small print run. Poetry Ireland/Éigse Éireann, Bermingham Tower, Dublin Castle, Dublin 2, Phone (01) 671 4632, may be able to advise you on that score. Éigse Éireann is funded by both Arts Councils to promote and encourage poetry throughout Ireland.

Print Run

If you are looking for advice on the number of books you should print for your first run, I would suggest between 750 and 1,000 if it is a book of poetry. You might consider the advice in the previous paragraph and go for an individually numbered limited edition.

A novel could have a print run of 2,000 and I would suggest a first print run of 3,000 copies for a biography of a well-known personality. If you are printing a local history I would recommend a first print run of 2,000.

With regard to second and subsequent print runs, this is a matter for you. I could not give any advice here as it will be based on the initial success of your first print run, the length of time that it took to sell out, the response of booksellers and the media publicity obtained.

Hardback Copies

By and large, a self-published book will only be produced in soft-back. Only if you reach the pinnacle of success of writers like Dermot Bolger (who started out

CHAPTER 2: Getting Sponsorship and Book Pricing

on his writing career by publishing his own work under the banner of Raven Arts Press) can you publish in hardback. However, if you can afford it, it is a good idea to get a couple of hundred hardback copies produced. The additional cost will easily be met by supplying the Library Service yourself (should they be interested in acquiring copies of your book) and by selling copies to friends or individuals who would like "a special copy".

When the book is being printed, ask the printer to leave about one hundred copies without covers and get him to run off about two or three hundred dust jackets. This the printer should be able to do at little or no extra cost. You can take the hundred copies and dust jackets home and get the books bound as money becomes available. If you live in the Leinster area I would recommend Duffy Bookbinders in Seville Place, Dublin 1, Phone (01) 874 1579. I have been using them since 1983 and have found the proprietor Tom Duffy to be a competent and sincere bookbinder who will complete your order to the highest standard. If you live outside Dublin, you can Fastrack your parcel to them. The cost per book will be in the region of £1.50 to £2 for a binding run of 200 copies and over, though prices will vary depending on the quantity required. Your retail price of the hardback edition should be between £5 and £7 greater than the softback price.

You can ask your printer for a price on one or two hundred hardback copies, and get a quote from a local bookbinder. Compare the estimates and make your choice. However, remember to get those extra dust-jackets, which can also be used to make up posters for sticking in shop windows, restaurants or in bus and train stations or business premises - it depends on your approach to the personnel in the various places whether you will get your posters displayed. I approached staff in Westland Row Railway Station and they kindly allowed me to display a few posters for "Confessions of a Court Clerk" and I displayed posters for "Dublin 7" in church porches, post offices and shops throughout the district. I displayed dust jackets for "Irish Lives" in Irish Clubs, libraries and youth hostels throughout Western Australia. Don't be shy to ask for your posters to be placed in locations that you frequent - your church, newsagent, pub or club. You will find that they will be only too happy to assist you.

Finally, you should keep a small number of dust jackets aside for the future - if you need additional hardback copies these can be made up from your softback stock without much difficulty.

CHAPTER 3

Critical Comments

How many books have you read with the comments of well-known journalists, critics, authors or prominent personalities on the back cover? It certainly adds to a book! You may consider seeking the comments of a few journalists. I have found the members of this profession to be very approachable, helpful and indeed eager to give a lift to a budding author. I would advise you to first communicate with a journalist that you regularly read. In my own case I generally seek the criticisms of Eanna Brophy in the Sunday Press, as I think my Sunday would not be the same without his column. I enjoy his page, he is a very witty and entertaining journalist - probably one of the wittiest in the country. I also regularly read Gene Kerrigan, who I first enjoyed through the pages of "Magill". Michael O'Toole, formerly of the 'Dubliners' Diary' page in the Evening Press and now with his own Thursday column, is another favourite of mine. His writing, "without fear or favour", is most entertaining and refreshing. Other journalists that I admire and have supplied quotes for my books include Kevin Myers and Matt Nugent.

I would suggest that you write to the journalists that you enjoy most, sending them a copy of your manuscript and seeking a few sentences for the cover. Their comments, appearing on the back of a book, do, I believe, enhance its standing and often add a bit of good humour into the bargain! You need not confine your quest for critical comments to journalists - you can approach published authors as well, but again, to be fair to them, you should be familiar with their work and preferably have a couple of their books on your shelf.

If you are writing a book of poetry you could approach a well-known poet; if it is a book on music you might ask a well-known DJ, Radio personality or musician

CHAPTER 3: *Critical Comments*

to give a comment; if it is a biography, a politician or clerical personality might be able to give an appropriate comment. If approaching a politician, you will probably find that one who represents your area would have the energy and interest to give it their best shot. If it is a audio cassette or compact disc the same might apply - an endorsement by a well-known personality would not go astray!

In any event, be inventive - see what will enhance your own particular book and go for it! Gabriel Rosenstock entered his novel "Lacertidae" for the Oireachtas Festival and one adjudicator admired the professionalism of the writing; the other said that it "definitely wasn't a novel" - whatever else it was. Rosenstock, humorously, used both comments on the blurb!

CHAPTER 4

ISBN Number

Nearly every publication nowadays has an ISBN, an International Book Serial Number and there is no mystery to getting such a number for your new publication. The process is simple - you just write off to Whitaker Book Information, Bibliographic Services, J Whitaker & Sons, 12, Dyott Street, London WC1A 1DF, Phone 071 836 8911, giving them the following information in writing:

(i) The name of the publisher/imprint as quoted on the book.

(ii) The full postal address of the publisher together with any telephone and fax numbers.

(iii) VAT number, if applicable.

(iv) Giro account number, if applicable.

(v) An estimate of how many different titles you (the publisher) are likely to produce in a twelve-month period.

(vi) A photocopy, or rough draft, of the title page and of the page which quotes the publisher.

The bar-code, which appears on everything these days - can be arranged by your typesetter or printer at no cost, for once they have the ISBN number, they can arrange the supply of a bar-code.

A free service, Whitaker Bibliographic Services lists the titles of publishers based in, or exporting English language titles into, Ireland and the UK; these include publishers from the US, Singapore, Hong Kong, India, China, Japan and many other countries. The UK is one of the most prolific publishing communities in the world and this is reflected in "Whitaker Books in Print".

CHAPTER 4: *ISBN Number*

Through associations with DW Thorpe, publisher of "Australia and New Zealand Books in Print" and with R R Bowker, your title is available to the massive markets of the USA and Australasia. Whitaker list in-print titles of over 70,000 publishers, including over 22,000 active European publishers. It is worthwhile noting that Whitaker services are used by booksellers and librarians in 106 countries, so a listing of your title will gain world-wide market notification. In addition Whitaker is the supplier of Cataloguing-in-Publication data to the British National Bibliographic Service.

Whitaker provide distribution details of all the titles received - a crucial listing insofar as the small publisher is concerned. Details include the publisher's and distributor's name, address, telephone and fax number. The data relating to your book can be amended at any time - just notify Whitaker; incidentally, they are introducing a Teleordering system, which means that orders can be automatically routed to any one of 22,000 distributors worldwide, including your own distributor - be it Eason's or yourself or next-door neighbour.

If you are reprinting your book, the same ISBN number will do; however, if you are republishing an amended edition of your book, or reprinting under a different publisher's name and address or new title, you will need a new ISBN number. Whitaker's have published an excellent guidebook on all aspects, including new editions, in their booklet "ISBN Incorporating Guidelines for Software Publishers" (ISBN 0 949999 07 5 Price £4.50).

If you wish to find out more about Whitaker, you can write to them for an information pack. They put on a 'Travelling Roadshow' every year which visits locations throughout the United Kingdom and all of Ireland. These are very informative exhibitions which gives one an amazing insight into the whole book industry. I attended one such information day in Buswell's Hotel, Kildare Street, Dublin, in May 1993 and learned a lot about the book world. As a matter of interest to the reader, they were able to tell me what books on self-publishing were issued, the type of publication and the retail cost.

There is no legal requirement to have an ISBN, nor does it affect copyright in any way. It is purely a convenience to the book trade and to librarians. The National Library in Kildare Street issues ISSN numbers, which relate to magazines.

CHAPTER 5

Copyright

Copyright is the exclusive right to the reproduction of a literary, artistic or other protected work, reproduction meaning publication, performance or broadcasting. Copyright belongs automatically to the creator of the work - you!. No formalities are necessary to establish copyright, which exists in anything originally created, including text, illustrations, diagrams, photographs and cover design. It is customary for evidential purposes to make a formal claim to copyright on a book by putting on the title verso (that is, the page after the title page), a declaration as follows:

© Copyright A N Other, Year of Publication.

The ownership of copyright lies with the author of the work, who may license another to reproduce the work in exchange for royalties. This is the normal form of a book publishing contract and should be noted should you be eventually successful in securing a publisher.

Copyright in the Republic of Ireland is governed by the Copyright Act, 1963, which was based by and large on the British Copyright Act of 1956. That Act lays down, following the International Copyright Convention, that copyright lasts for the lifetime of the author and for fifty years thereafter. It is important that you consult the Act in order to comply with all your legal requirements - you can obtain a copy from the Government Publications Sales Office, Sun Alliance House, Molesworth Street, Dublin 2, Phone (01) 671 0309, price £6.90, postage 75p extra.

Copyright in Northern Ireland is governed by the Copyright, Design and Patents Act, 1988. This Act is rather complicated, as I discovered when I first read it; however, you will just have to plough through it and see what requirements you will have to meet. You can buy a copy of the Act, price £12, from the HMSO, Government Bookshop, 80, Chichester Street, Belfast, Phone (0232) 238451.

CHAPTER 5: *Copyright*

Alternatively, you can call in to the Linenhall Library in Belfast, Phone (0232) 321707, and consult a copy of the Act there, free of charge.

To support a claim for breach of copyright in the Courts in the USA, a formal deposit must have been made in the Library of Congress.

Deposit Copies

You will have to lodge some copies of your book with a number of Libraries in order to satisfy your legal requirements under Section 56(i) of the Copyright Act, 1963, which basically requires the publisher of every book first published in the State to leave a total of thirteen copies of the book with the following agencies within one month of such publication:

1. Copyright Section, National Library, Kildare St., Dublin 2 (one copy);

2. Copyright Section, British Library, 2, Sheraton Street, London WIV 4BH (one copy);

3. Copyright Section, National University of Ireland, Merrion Square, Dublin 2 (four copies - one each for UCD, UCC, UCG and Maynooth);

4. Copyright Section, The Library, Trinity College, Dublin 2 (one copy);

5. Irish Copyright Agency, The Library, Trinity College, Dublin 2 (four copies - only if demanded, within twelve months of publication, for the copyright libraries in Britain; they will request copies in writing if required);

6. Acquisitions Librarian, Dublin City University, Glasnevin, Dublin 9 (one copy) and

7. Acquisitions Librarian, University of Limerick, Plassey Technological Park, Limerick (one copy).

Finally, the Irish Copyright Licensing Agency at 19, Parnell Square, Dublin 1, licenses schools and colleges to photocopy in quantity and arrange for collection and payment of royalties accordingly.

International Listing

It is most important from the marketing aspect that you furnish copies of your book to the National Library and the British Museum Library irrespective of your

CHAPTER 5: *Copyright*

compulsion to do so by law, as these institutions will place your title on an International listing. Your copies to both these institutions must be "finished and coloured in the same manner as the best copies .... and on the best paper". In other words, if you publish a small number of hardback editions, then you must send them in a hardback copy. The copies to the other institutions need only be your ordinary paperback copies.

You may overlook this important matter of depositing copies of your book in order to comply with the laws relating to copyright, but it is worthwhile knowing that the National Library of Ireland endeavour to acquire a copy of all printed material relating to the whole of Ireland. Very frequently, it holds the only copy of such material, which is readily available to the public. Indeed, the National Library is probably the most important information source for anyone contemplating research of any kind. However, it is entitled to a copy of every piece of material published so you are obliged by law to send them in a copy of your book. If by any chance you forget to do so, the efficient National Library staff will probably send you a request for a copy of your book.

In any event it is in your own best interests to get a copy of your book to them as quickly as possible, as the National Library has responsibility for the compilation and publication of the "Irish Publishing Record", an annual listing of Irish publications produced in the whole of Ireland. The "Irish Publishing Record" is purchased by libraries and institutions worldwide and so provides valuable free publicity for your material. So by complying with the Copyright Act you are, in the process, getting free publicity for your book.

EU Legislation

Finally, there are obligations arising from membership of the EU (formerly the EEC) which requires compliance with EU regulations, directives and legislation. In this regard you can contact the European Commission Information Office, 43, Molesworth Street, Dublin 2, Phone (01) 671 9100 and Windsor House, 9/15 Bedford Street, Belfast BT2 7EG, Phone 44323. Their library is open to the public and you can go in and check out all their data relating to European copyright.

Typesetting and origination

courtesy of

CHAPTER 6

Typesetting and Printing

Typesetting is something that can nowadays be done in the home with the modern array of Personal Computers available coupled with the advent of Desktop publishing. I use a Wang PC350 and find it can meet all of my modest publishing needs. However, you may not have the facility on your PC to complete what is called a camera-ready copy of your work. In that event you will need to go to your printer or typesetter with your disk, who will then transfer it over to their in-house system, complete the lay-out and prepare the text for printing. Have the document on your disc proof-read and ready for printing before sending it to the typesetter or printer.

Free-lance experts who can put your manuscript in shape, from start to finish, frequently advertise in "Books Ireland" (Phone (01) 269 2185), should you feel that the advice given in this book is a little too daunting for you, and if you have the funds to avail of their services (which I never had). Some books, for instance, may require indexing - a terrible job that may be better left to the experts! You can also check your Yellow Pages under the heading "Designers - Advertising and Graphics".

Even if you have the facilities to finalise your book for the printer, I feel that you will definitely need to go to a typesetter in order to get the cover designed. There is nothing like a professionally designed cover - after all, it is the cover which will sell your book in the end, as it is the cover that the punter sees on the bookshelves! So a couple of hundred pounds handed over to a typesetter to design the artwork for the cover of your book will not go astray. Indeed, it will be the best investment that you are likely to make on your book. Whether you go for a full-colour, two-colour or single-colour cover, it is definitely worthwhile to get the professionals to carry out the actual design.

CHAPTER 6: *Typesetting and Printing*

Cover Design

A good, well-designed cover is one of the most important aspects of your book, as an attractive presentation is necessary in order to catch the eye of the consumer. Your book will also be vying with hundreds of other titles for shelf space in the bookshops, so an eye-catching cover will help in this regard. Designing the cover should cost you in the region of £60 to £150, depending on whether it is a full-colour or two-colour cover and is a solid investment in the overall success of your book. If your book is going to retail at under £4, then I would suggest a two-colour cover; if it will cost £4.95 or more I would recommend a full-colour cover. However, the printer will give you your estimate for the job with both a full-colour and a two-colour cover and you can then decide if you can afford the difference. Don't forget, the printer can reverse the print to give you three colours on the cover, making it quite attractive.

Occasionally a painting or a detail of a painting from one of the art galleries may fit the bill for your front cover design. You can try the souvenir shop in any Art Gallery or Museum for a suitable print or picture postcard. Check the copyright requirements if you are thinking of using such prints for your book. You may wish to put your portrait on the back cover and if so, a good, clear photograph should fit the bill.

There are many artists, such as Robert Ballagh, Pieter Sluis and Annie Siggins, and a host of free-lance designers, whose services can be availed of to design and draft your front cover, if you have a generous budget - see "Books Ireland" for their advertisements or consult your Golden or Yellow Pages. For my own requirements I have been using Typeform, Newtown Industrial Estate, Clonshaugh, Dublin 17, Phone (01) 847 5822, to design and layout my books during the past number of years. I have not only been very happy with, but have enjoyed, their attitude to my work. They have taken it on board and sometimes I thought that the book was *their* creation, such was their genuine enthusiasm for the project.

I published a small book of poetry in June 1993 by the pupils of Scoil Oilibhéir, in Blanchardstown, entitled 'Seoda Óga'. I was kindly presented with a sketch by Don Conroy, the well-known children's author, for the cover. I approached Typeform and they designed the cover for me. The cost was fully worth it - the cover was widely admired and helped to get the small book shelf space in many leading bookstores - a good achievement for a book of poetry by young National school pupils!

With regard to the paper type for your cover, you will need a good-quality board. If your book has a full-colour cover, I would recommend a glossy board; if it is a two-colour or three-colour cover, I might go for a matt finish; however, seek the advice of your printer in this regard.

Finally, if your book is being published during a special year, such as the 1988 Dublin Millennium, Mayo 800, Newry 850, Galway 500 or Armagh Together 1994-1995, you should try and get approval to incorporate the logo on your cover. I was told that the logo of "Dublin - European City of Culture 1991" on my book "Waiting for the 22", added a touch of quality to the production.

Photographs

If your book has a load of photographs you would be better off letting a typesetter handle all the artwork. They can transfer photographs directly onto a screen with the latest technology, saving considerably on negatives and bromides. If they have the text on screen, it will be easy for them to insert the photographs in suitably identified slots throughout the book. It would be most cost-effective to let the typesetter produce the camera-ready copy in the event of your having a lot of photographs and illustrations.

No Name Publications

You may wish to put a publisher trade name on your book instead of using your own name. This will not only enhance your publication but will also give you a better shot at getting reviews, as the media tend to be a little bit shy of a book with the author's name appearing as the publisher. Your cover designer can create a logo for your chosen trade name at little or no extra cost. You can register your trade name with the Companies Office for a fee of £15. You may need to do this in order to have any cheques made payable to the trade name processed by the

clearing banks. Forms can be obtained from the Registrar of Companies, Companies Registration Office, Dublin Castle, Dublin 2, Phone (01) 661 4222. There is no similar registration facility available in Northern Ireland - you will have to go for a full-blown Limited Company. Contact the Registry of Companies, Credit Unions and Industrial & Provident Societies, IDB House, 64, Chichester Street, Belfast 1, Phone (0232) 234488 for information.

CHAPTER 6: *Typesetting and Printing*

Printing

Printing a book nowadays needn't be the headache it once was. If you have a well-presented, camera-ready copy you will only need two visits to the printer in order to finalise details. The better prepared your material, the less call upon you for advice by the printer.

If you live in Dublin, I would strongly recommend Futureprint Limited of Baldoyle, Dublin 13, Phone (01) 839 2070, having availed of their services since my second book "North of the Liffey - A Character Sketchbook", in 1984. Indeed, since then they have printed all my titles. They are very professional and because they specialise in books are most competitive. Their staff are very patient with the novice and will go through your requirements in detail, adding in their own suggestions along the way. They are also most reliable and will always deliver the product on time. In addition they provide a typesetting service and so can quote you an all-in competitive rate. As all the functions would then be carried out in-house, the cost would be less than if you went to a typesetter separately. Again, if you have your manuscript on disk and already proof-read, considerable savings will be made in this area. No matter how small your requirements, contact Paul Bolger in their Book Publishing Advisory Service unit.

If you live in the Belfast region, competitive influences come into play and you should consult your Yellow Pages for details of printers and typesetters. Always seek at least three quotations - it's a free service. Again, you may consider giving Futureprint a ring for a quote - they can arrange delivery of the final product to you anywhere in Ireland.

Proofs

Before proceeding to the printing stage, the printer will show you the proofs for your approval. This is the most important stage of the whole process, as this will result in the finished product. Check the proofs carefully. If you have photographs or sketches included, make sure that they are all in their right place and check each caption - if you have them - carefully.

Country Location

If you live in or near a provincial town, the local newspaper could be approached with regard to your printing requirements. An excellent local history of Naas was expertly printed by the Leinster Leader a couple of years ago and if you examine the bookshelves of your own local bookshop you might see some

CHAPTER 6: *Typesetting and Printing*

examples of the printing assignments of your local newspaper or printer. It might be no harm to get two other estimates, if this is possible, from printers in your area before you approach your local paper so that you have something to work on.

When you have got your figures, I would advise you to telephone Futureprint, giving them full details of your requirements. They will ring you back with their quote, or post it out to you. Futureprint will deliver your book to you anywhere in Ireland.

If your local newspaper or printer is carrying out your printing, I would still advise you to consider communicating with Typeform by post with regard to your cover design - the very efficient postal service eliminates the need for personal visitation. If the process becomes urgent for any reason, you can use the Express mail service. I have used this form of communication with Typeform on many occasions and have found it to be secure as well as fast.

Finally, you should give your printer a deadline date of at least one week before your launch for delivery of your book, otherwise you will find that the deadline they will work to is the launch date. In this way you will have your book in plenty of time to drop copies into a couple of chosen journalists and to enclose one copy of the book with your Press Release to the various media news-desks.

Binding

There are numerous forms of book binding, such as stitch, perfect and staple binding. The most expensive of these forms is stitch binding. This process involves the stitching of sections of the book together which are then glued to the cover. This form of binding would be necessary for books which would be subjected to a lot of wear and tear, like enclyopedias and school text-books. The next form is called perfect binding, where the book is glued together and the spine is milled away before gluing the book onto it. The last, and cheapest form of binding, is staple binding, where the book is stapled onto the spine.

The size of the book does not dictate the type of binding required - it is the quality demanded. Perfect binding is the most popular form and generally most books are produced with this form of binding. However, if you have a small book of local history, a short story or a book of poetry running to between 40 to 60 pages and your budget is limited, I would recommend staple binding. I have used this form on two recent publications and it certainly did not diminish the quality of the books. The form of binding chosen should be discussed with your printer taking into account the desired quality of the finished product, the full cost of publishing and the budget available to you.

Finally, a new form of binding, called "Burst Binding", has been introduced, whereby perforations are done in the paper folding before gluing. The book is then glued to a spine, which is not milled away as in the perfect binding process. This form of binding gives the strength of stitch-binding, less the expense.

Paper Type

Paper quality is a very important factor insofar as the overall quality of your book is concerned and the paper to be used will depend on the image you want to project and the type of publication you are producing. There is a wide variety of different paper stocks available in a diverse choice of substances, which can give an enormous range of "feel" to your publication - a very important aspect of book publishing. The type of paper also depends on the way you want the final product to look and on the particular market you are aiming at. Here are some guidelines on suitable paper type:

Bookwove: An uncoated, bulky paper which comes in various substances and "volume". This latter term refers to the thickness of the sheet. Most bookwoves are either vellum or slightly off-white in shade. I would recommend bookwove for all novels, as it is the most economical paper available and is in more common use.

Matt coated: A matt coated paper which is available in a wide range of substances, suitable for educational, local history or poetry books. This paper is ideal if you are using photographs in your publication.

Gloss art: A gloss coated woodfree sheet which is very suitable for illustrations but tends nowadays not to be specified for large areas of type.

These are just three examples of the type of papers that are available. There is no hard and fast rule regarding which paper is most suitable for a particular publication. To get the best advice I would suggest that you consult with a reputable paper merchant.

Mc Naughton Paper Ireland Limited, 67, Cherry Orchard Industrial Estate, Dublin 20, Phone (01) 626 1601 and 8, Duncrue Road, Belfast BT3 9BP, Phone (0232) 774004 carry an extensive range of various types of paper in a variety of colours and substances. They would be only too willing to discuss your requirements and will even make up a dummy book for you to give you some

CHAPTER 6: *Typesetting and Printing*

idea on how your finished product will look. Mc Naughton's can take your order and deliver the paper to wherever your printer operates from.

If in Need of a Reprint

If your book takes off and you need to get further copies reprinted, additional copies can be run off by your printer. Remember, a reprint is going to cost you a lot less than the original run, as you will not have the associated typesetting, lay-out, photograph and camera-copy expenses. When ordering your reprint, remember to insert the words "Reprinted 19??" beside the original date of publication. This is important, not least in securing additional publicity for the reprint, as it is your proof that the first print run was sold out!

Elizabeth Ferris

<u>SOLICITOR</u>

Arran Chambers,
6 Arran Quay, Dublin 7.

Telephone: 8721455/8721091
Answer Phone: 8721455 Fax: 8721091

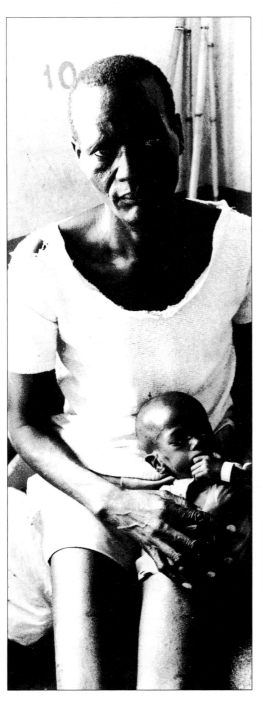

OUR GOAL IS TO HELP

Help us to fight disease and injustice in the Third World. GOAL is the sport's enthusiast's charity. GOAL scores against poverty.

John O'Shea,
GOAL, P.O. Box 19,
Dun Laoghaire, Co. Dublin.
Tel: 280 9779
Fax: 280 9215

CHAPTER 7

The Launch

At last the big day is approaching - the occasion you have been waiting for! Your book launch is one of the most important aspects of your whole effort, as by and large, a good launch will ensure the commercial success of your book because the publicity from it will certainly get you good shelf space in some of the large bookshops and could help you in securing a distributor. There are three steps to take with regard to arranging your launch - deciding the actual date, choosing the venue and then inviting the press and guests.

Autumn Leaves

What time of the year should you launch your book? Any time between early October and very early December - in order for you to catch the Christmas market, when 65% of all books are sold. I launched "Confessions of a Court Clerk" in June 1989. Despite plenty of publicity and a slot on the Pat Kenny Radio Show, by November of that year I had sold only 200 copies. I had long since used up all my marketing opportunities and was facing a massive disaster! Tom Owens of Easons rang me up in mid-November and asked me to take the returns. Imagine my shock when I discovered that he was talking about 1,500 copies.

I asked him to hold on to them for another six weeks and he very kindly agreed. I wrote to the Sunday Press Editor and asked for a write-up in the circumstances, citing my regular readership of the SP. I also wrote to Michael O'Toole in the Diary, Evening Press, telling him of my desperate situation. Following a kind mention in the Diary in late November and in the SP in early December, I had a phone call from Tom Owens stating that the book was moving. In April 1990 I was furnished with the returns - a mere three hundred copies. Only for the goodwill of the SP and EP towards a regular customer of theirs, I would still be paying back my Credit Union loan on "Confessions of a Court Clerk". So your launch will have to be in the October to December period to enjoy any sort of commercial success.

CHAPTER 7: *The Launch*

We have the best time of year, now for the best hour of the day, which is between 6 and 7pm in the evening. This will ensure you the publicity you need and also a good turnout - invitees can drop in on their way home from work if they have something else on. However, the key reason for the suitability of this time is the fact that you need to get journalists to attend and report on your launch. Have it at 8 or 9pm, and journalists will be busy enjoying themselves at earlier functions and might not bother to leave to cover yours. More than likely they will have covered enough functions and at 8 or 9pm they will be back in their office, busy writing up their Diary page or social column. So it has to be an early evening affair!

Venue

The important thing here is to match your venue to the book. If it is a local history, or a book of poetry of a purely local flavour, then definitely go for a local launch. If your book is of a general nature, then a city-centre or town-centre location, convenient for journalists, is recommended. My only advice to you on this aspect of your project is not to pay for a room - get a publican, hotelier or community/sports centre or Social Club Manager to sponsor your launch. You will find that they will be more than willing in this regard. If not, look for a venue that won't cost you anything.

If your venue is a pub, they should be happy to provide the savories - cheese on crackers, cocktail sausages and the like - free of charge. The modest outlay to them will be more than offset by the alcoholic and soft drink merchandise sold during the night. If the venue cannot furnish free savories, then see if your local restaurant will do it for you in return for a small advertisement in your book and distribution of their menu on the night of the launch.

In my own case, I have launched books in Hanlon's pub (Hanlon's Corner, North Circular Road) the Alfie Byrne pub (Four Courts), Mc Grath's pub (Fassaugh Avenue, Cabra West), Giraffes Play Centre (Coolmine - a children's indoor play arena), the Parish Centre, Cabra West and the five-star Langley Hotel, Perth, Western Australia. Hanlons, Giraffes, Alfie Byrne's and the Langley Hotel provided the savories free of charge, while the popular northside bistro Brams & Liszt, Santry, provided the savories in Mc Grath's and the Parish Centre. In all the venues invitees were particularly impressed by the standard and presentation of the food, thus ensuring a good return by way of patronising from those attending the launch. Remember, the locations are going to benefit from your publicity - Michael O Toole paid glowing tribute to Hanlon's pint of "Bud" in his Evening Press column, and their business no doubt benefited from the compliment!

CHAPTER 7: *The Launch*

Even the prestigious locations are not immune to providing free facilities for a book launch - I attended the launch of Shane O Doherty's "The Immaculate Deception" in the Shelbourne Hotel, on Dublin's St Stephen's Green and the facilities there were provided to Shane free of charge.

Another type of venue which you may consider is your local Arts Centre, which would more than likely be only too happy to provide the venue - for example the Old Museum Arts Centre in College Square North, Belfast, is popular as a venue for book-launchings. Your Arts Centre can probably only provide a room and if this is so take my advice above and try and get a cafe or restaurant to provide the wine and savories as suggested; consult your Golden or Yellow pages for the address of your local Arts Centre.

Who to Invite

Get nice invitation cards printed and send one to everybody you know or can think of! Speedy Print, situated at 224 Parnell Street, Dublin 1, Phone (01) 872 1807, produce a fine invitation card at short notice and little expense. It is worthwhile remembering that in the busy lifestyles that we all now lead in the First World, a lot of people might be unable to attend your launch. So invite as many as you can think of. If you invite 300, you will be lucky to get 150 present. If you do get the full 300, don't worry - it is now too late and worrying will do you no good! A healthy attendance will add to the atmosphere and give the launch a party flavour - encouraging journalists present to hang on for the craic!

There are certain people you will need to invite and the most important in this regard are the book-buyers, the most important being those employed at the major bookshops in your own city, town or region. For example, if it is a Dublin launch, invite the book buyers in the following shops: Easons (O'Connell Street, ILAC and Irish Life Centre), Fred Hanna, Hannas (Rathmines), Hodges Figgis, Greenes, Waterstones and Webbs and Veritas. If the book has any religious aspect, invite the book buyer of your own leading religious shops. Do not forget to invite the proprietors of whatever local outlets you have lined up to sell your book.

CHAPTER 7: *The Launch*

More than likely book buyers will be unable to attend - after all, this is their busiest time of year. However, inviting them will put your book in mind, they will watch out for any media reaction and they will be the ones providing the shelf-space for your work. So it is important to remember them. You will also need to invite the Chief Purchasing Officer or Stocks Editor of your Library Service/s and your local Library staff. Again, they might not attend but at least they will know the title of your book should any reader request a copy in their Library.

You might also wish to invite your local community leaders - representatives from the various clubs, your particular church, Community Council members, Credit Union officials, your bank staff. Your work colleagues and officials of your Union are another group you should not forget - you will be looking for a mention in the Union magazine afterwards! It is worthwhile remembering that politicians might like to be asked to attend, especially if the book is a local history or of a well-known personality. The presence of politicians give a launch a party (with a small p) or celebrity flavour, and this in turn helps with getting a write-up in the papers. So inviting politicians works both ways: they get the publicity and mix with their constituents and you get the party swinging and the photographs in the newspapers.

Other invitees could include the teachers in whatever schools you attended, a representative from your local police station, local businesses and anyone who helped you along the way. The more people you have at the launch, the more your book will be talked about - word of mouth also helps to sell your book! Finally, your local Arts Centre may be able to provide you with a list of names of suitable persons "in the business" that you could consider inviting to your launch.

Press Release

About eight or ten days before the launch, you should send out a suitable Press Release, *running to no more than one page,* setting out the details of your book in brief, your own brief background and any other relevant material. If your Press Release runs to two or more pages and contains a bountiful supply of waffle, it will end up in the bin. KISS is the operative word here - **K**eep **I**t **S**hort and **S**imple! The Press Release should be directed to:

The Editor, Newsdesk, (Name of Publication or Radio/TV Station).

If you have copies of your book available, it would be a good idea to send it out with each Press Release.

Important advice with regard to your launch: it is no harm to hire a photographer for the occasion, or enlist the services of a friend if they are good with a camera. In cases where the media do not turn up, suitable photographs coupled with a written article by yourself covering the launch could be circulated to newspapers and in magazines and would hopefully result in some coverage. You can push the local newspapers for coverage in this way, as they may not be able to send a photographer to cover your launch. Any publicity thus earned would have more than covered the modest cost of photography. In addition, invitees are delighted to receive copies of photographs of the reception as a memento.

Stay Clear

On the night of your launch I would advise you to stay well clear of the sales point of your book, otherwise you will be caught up in the act of selling your book, giving change or looking after any monies received. Get a couple of friends, or better still, a shop assistant or two that you may know, set up a table and let them handle your book sales on their own. Pay them for their services at the end of the night. This advice is most important as you need to be left free to sign books and give any interviews to the press that may be required of you. Don't forget this important hint - stay well clear of your sales table!

VIP

Finally, on the night, you may get carried away on an infectious cloud of euphoria. If you do, well and good, but remember one golden rule - don't forget the journalists! When I launched "Irish Lives" in the Langley Hotel in Perth, there was a tremendous atmosphere in the room. The Irish Ambassador to Australia launched the book and there were many prominent personalities from the Australian/Irish community present. The craic was ninety. I was in the middle of a crowd chatting away when someone said to me that a journalist from the "West Australian", the leading State newspaper, wanted to talk to me. I said that I would be with him in a minute and continued with my conversation.

Less than a minute later the journalist tipped me on the shoulder, introduced himself to me and said "I'm off now". I immediately left my company and asked him to allow me a couple of minutes. "Listen, you don't keep a journalist waiting. I have work to do. I was going to leave without telling you, so I was doing you a favour letting you know I was going. Other journalists might not. You do not keep a journalist waiting - they are the most important people at your launch. Look after them and then give your time to your other guests".

CHAPTER 7: *The Launch*

It was a cheap lesson, for luckily, he did the interview with me and I got my write-up in the West Australian - a whole page on St Patrick's Day! Ever since then I have given my full attention to journalists and then I relax and enjoy the launch, mingling with all the guests. So remember, put the journalist first - seek them out, look after them and then enjoy yourself. An important hint also in this regard - treat all journalists the same; do not leave a journalist waiting because he or she is "only" from a local newspaper or if the interviewer is "only" from Radio Anna Livia and not RTE. No matter where they come from, any journalist is your VIP and treat them all equally. Keep that in mind and you will never go wrong!

CHAPTER 8

Distribution

The most critical part of your whole project - it is no good getting publicity for your book in all the newspapers in the land and plenty of Radio coverage if it is not on the shelf when the consumer decides to purchase. You must get your book into all bookshops, or as many as you can, in tandem with your reviews.

Distribution is something that any self-publisher will have to think hard about. Even if your book is of a very local nature, you will still need to get it into bookshops. When I wrote "Waiting for the 22" I was advised to use just local sales outlets. Because of the book's very local content - a celebration of the first fifty years of the parish of Cabra West (the best place in the world) - I was told that the book would only sell within the confines of the district. I had already secured local outlets in the Post Office, the Church Repository Shop, Londis Supermarket, Johnny's the shoemakers and the First National Building Society.

However, following a meeting with Mr Tom Owens of Eason & Son, I decided to take the experienced advice and gave them most of my copies to distribute. Over 60% of the first (and only) print run of 3,000 copies were distributed through Easons. They sold the book through all their own outlets and distributed it to shops as far apart as Galway, Sligo, Cork and Belfast! In June 1993 I got an order from Easons for thirty copies of the book - eighteen months after the launch - so much for a book of purely local interest! In these days of a highly mobile society, there is no such thing as a book of purely local interest. So a good distribution plan is necessary for the success of your book.

Importance of Distributor

A distributor is most important for the commercial success of your book and whenever a newspaper article on your book catches the eye of a reader, your product has to be readily available from that reader's local newsagent. If the local newsagent has not got it in stock, a phone call to your distributor will get it to the shop and another customer is happy. One thing is certain, you cannot effectively

CHAPTER 8: *Distribution*

distribute the book yourself. Imagine getting an order for three copies from Eason's in Tallaght, four copies from Hanna's in Rathmines and three copies from Roselawn Bookstore in Blanchardstown! You have to get the book into the three shops promptly, invoice them and chase up the invoices - a time-consuming and sometimes frustrating effort.

Eason's

Recommendations in this regard: Easons, Brickfield Drive, Dublin 12, Phone (01) 453 6211 and Boucher Road, Belfast, Phone (0232) 381200. I have availed of their distribution services since my first book back in 1983. I have found them to be reliable, honest, efficient and helpful. In 1985 I was approached by a distributor requesting sole distribution rights to my book "Lugs - the Life and Times of Jim Branigan". I was presented with a package that included the distributor printing posters and advertising the book. Cautiously, I gave about 300 books along with 250 copies of "A History of Cabra and Phibsborough", which had also been requested. Pressed by them, I refused to hand over sole distribution rights and following discussions with Tom Owens I subsequently gave Eason's all copies of all my books for distribution. A couple of months later the particular Dublin outfit went into liquidation, leaving me unpaid. It was a cheap lesson for me, for I have never received a penny for the books and some of those involved in that distribution network are still in the book business. However, I could have been persuaded to give everything and be still paying back a Credit Union loan to cover my losses. So I was lucky!

As a result of this experience, I would only use Eason's Distributors and accordingly they are the only company I can recommend. With regard to payment, Eason's are a big fish and bookshops will settle accounts promptly with them; a major player in the book industry, if they are handling *your* book they will be looking for prompt payment from the shops. No matter that your book is a small affair - if shops sell it, Eason's want to be paid for it and because they supply such a large part of a bookshop's merchandise, settlement of accounts is the order of the day. It is well worth the cost.

Weekly Listing

Easons place your book on a listing which is sent out to all bookshops every Friday. In addition, it may be included in a well-presented, up-market books catalogue which they periodically publish. In this way you book is enjoying added publicity and is kept in the minds of booksellers.

CHAPTER 8: *Distribution*

I have always found Eason's to be more than efficient in settling their account - they thought nothing of making payments to me whenever I was requested to make stage payments to the printer or typesetter. Just a phone call to them and a cheque was forwarded in the post a few days later. Eason's charge 50% of the cost price of a book for their distribution services. It is a lot, but remember, you have only one account to handle and you are dealing with a professional outfit who will pay all their bills promptly. This in itself is money in the bank. Remember that the charge for shops is between 33% and 35%, depending on what you can work out with the individual stores. Of course, you then have the problem of chasing up each and every outlet for monies owed and postage expenses on books ordered by provincial bookshops or by bookshops far away from your home base.

You might not have much storage space in your home and if this is the case, and if the distributor says that they are only prepared to take a certain number, press them to go that little bit further. If the distributor requests 500, ask for that to be upped to 700. If they ask for 1,000 or 2,000, press them to take an extra three or four hundred. This will save you blocking up your sitting room with boxes of books.

Finally, there is the added bonus of enlisting the experience, help and support of people like Declan Heeney and Robin Gourley, Distribution Managers of Eason & Sons Dublin and Belfast respectively. Having their expertise and skill at your disposal is well worth the extra 17%. As in the case of supplying books to retail outlets, books are received on a "sale or return" basis.

What to Do

As soon as you have completed your manuscript, send a copy to a distributor, together with a covering letter, asking them to consider distributing your book. Follow-up your letter by telephone and try and arrange a meeting, as you will probably be better able to sell yourself in person. Try and secure a distributor before your book goes to the printer so that, if successful in your efforts, you can give the name and phone number of the distributor on the back cover and in the acknowledgements page.

CHAPTER 8: *Distribution*

If you don't secure a distributor at this stage, don't panic! All is not lost and as you are only entering the book world, do not be surprised if you have no success and don't be put off if Eason's decline to handle your book - tens of thousands of titles are published each year, making it impossible for any distributor to take every publication on board. In addition, there is a possibility that for marketing or logistical (or even legal) reasons a distributor may not be prepared to take on your book.

A Good Launch Helps

If your launch was successful from the point of view of publicity, this may encourage the major shops to take some copies of your book and a distributor may also be inclined to take your book on board. If you were unsuccessful in securing shop sales or a distributor in the pre-launch stage, it would be useful to make an appointment with some of the book-buyers and a distributor following your launch. Bring all press cuttings relating to your book and see if your publicity results in a change of heart. If it does not, don't worry, as you can bite the bullet and do the job yourself. It is hard going but very satisfying and rewarding. I brought the press cuttings relating to my first book "A History of Cabra and Phibsborough" into all the bookshops in town. I managed to twist the arm of the book-buyer in Eason's in O Connell Street. She said she would take five copies - I then gave her ten! She ordered more in stages until they were taking two hundred at a time. So the press cuttings worked!

No Distributor?

If you havn't a distributor, it is most important that you put your address and telephone contact number on the acknowledgements page and phone number on the back cover, so that anyone seeking a copy (or further copies) of your book will know where to contact. This is crucial and will help sell your book. If you have not got a phone, use a friend's or relative's telephone number.

Self-distribution is a hard road but in many ways is most rewarding. I could not secure a distributor for my first book "A History of Cabra and Phibsborough", where my choice of outlets included two local businesses, the local post office and standing outside the various local parish churches at weekends and travelling from pub to pub throughout the district. Look around your own locality to identify suitable outlets - for example if your old school has a shop, place some copies there.

CHAPTER 8: *Distribution*

You may be disheartened at first, but keep plugging away. Persistence in this regard does pay off. Eason's shop in O Connell Street was the first city-centre bookshop to order "A History of Cabra and Phibsborough" from me - they requested five copies! I pestered them to take ten. They next ordered twenty-five copies and I pestered them to take fifty! I went to every bookshop in the city with a copy of the book, pressing them, cajoling them, begging them: "even take just five copies". It is very hard work and you have to push very hard in order to get the shops to take some books, and even at that you then have to push them and project your product in order to get some display space. Keep plugging away and do not get disheartened!

One thing I found when I published my first book, "A History of Cabra and Phibsborough", and that was that a couple of the big shops were very slow in settling accounts, probably because I was such a small fish. One prominent store (not Eason's) left me waiting for over twelve months before settling an account. I ended up telling them that I was giving a Radio interview and would mention the fact that I still remained unpaid and would name them. My accounts were promptly settled.

Important advice if you are distributing yourself: supply your outlets with an invoice and get someone there to sign a copy invoice as receipt; secondly, if you are selling in pubs or outside the church or a community centre, and if it is going bad, do not be tempted to sell a copy to the odd punter who says "I'll give you a pound for one". Ignore them and keep trying. Give one such punter a book out of desperation and your credibility is gone. Believe me, no one else will buy your book unless it is going for a pound (or £2 as the case may be).

If you think of trying to sell your work at the Book Barrow Fair in the Mansion House I would advise that you give it a miss. It is really only for antiquarian or old books and you may not cover your costs for the day. I tried it once; I rented my stall and took up position at 9am one Monday morning. I did not cover the cost of my stall until 7pm that night. I just about covered my daily costs at the end of a long day of trading at 9pm. To be fair to the organisers, they *did* warn me that it was for rare and older books and would not be a suitable outlet for me, but I choose to ignore their expert advice.

You should try the pubs on Thursday and Friday nights, when people have some change in their pockets. Many writers have succeeded by just bringing a satchel around with them on Thursday and Friday nights to various pubs. Secure the permission of the bar-person in charge. Other writers like to target certain areas at certain times of the year, tapping the Rose of Tralee Festival, the City of Belfast

39

CHAPTER 8: *Distribution*

Horticultural Fair or the Galway Races and Oyster Festivals. For a detailed listing of the organisers of the various festivals throughout the country contact the Irish Writers' Centre. For details of fairs and festivals in Northern Ireland contact the Northern Ireland Tourist Board, 59, North Street, Belfast, Phone (0232) 233228 and 16, Nassau Street, Dublin 2, Phone (01) 679 1977.

There are also Gaelic football, rugby and soccer matches, Royal Down, Leopardstown and other horse racing events, carnivals and fairs; this is a brave way to sell your life's dreams and on the way you can make some new friends. The best of luck to you!

Put it Away

A good piece of advice here - put away all monies from your sales immediately. You would not see a fiver going here for a meal, another going there for a couple of pints and a tenner going on petrol. Before you know where you are, you will have to pay your book bills out of the housekeeping money, and as the printer will need to be paid within whatever time agreed, be it a month or six weeks or even two months, you will need every penny you take in.

If you have published your book under your own name, then open up a Deposit Account in your local Allied Irish Bank branch and regularly lodge all monies received - even if it is only a pound or two! Remember the money is not yours until you have paid all your bills. You can get cheques to pay all your creditors from the AIB at charges that are just a fraction of those you would incur with a current account.

If you have published under a trade name, you will have to open a business account in order to facilitate the clearing of cheques for payment of books received. Do not be tempted into opening a current account in the bank, where you will have a business cheque book to flash around. You might only carry out a half-dozen transactions and be paying £25 or more in bank fees. As stated above, an AIB Deposit Account will meet all your banking needs. Consult your phone book for your nearest AIB branch.

Finally, AIB can offer very attractive loans should you find yourself under pressure to clear your bills before adequate funds are to hand from book sales. This is something which you would want to seriously consider and can talk it over with your local AIB branch manager. You may be able to secure a loan for your project and pay all your bills up front, thereby relieving you of the pressure of having to sell your books in a short time span.

CHAPTER 8: *Distribution*

Supplying the Library Service

I have recommended that you get a number of hardback copies run-off. You can use some hardback copies as presentation gifts to those who helped you, for the comment writers featured on the back cover of your book, the foreword writer, the launch-person, your local Bank Manager or Credit Union Administrator. The rest can hopefully be supplied to the Library Service.

It is a matter for the Library Service itself whether they take your book. However, if you get a good burst of publicity and your book is receiving many requests from the general readership in various libraries, they will be interested. Supply the Library Service yourself; the discount to them is usually 10% to 15%; however, I generally offer a discount of 25% to 30% as I have a soft spot for the service, which is a free University of Learning that has, in southern Ireland, unfortunately been cut-back by well-heeled politicians who provide the best in terms of education to their own offspring. A generous discount also means that the Library Service can buy a couple of more copies of your book and 75% of the cost price of a hardback copy is not a bad return for you. The more that people borrow your book from a library, the more people are talking about it on the street, leading to the possibility of more sales.

When you have a few hardback copies to hand send one with a covering letter and home and work telephone number, to the Chief Purchasing Officer of the Library Service in your region. Don't forget that in Dublin there are now four Chief Purchasing Officers, for Dunlaoghaire/Rathdown, Fingal, South Dublin County Council and Dublin Corporation. The offices of the various divisions have not yet been finalised. As I go to print, Muiris O Reilly, Chief Purchasing Officer for Dunlaoghaire/Rathdown, is based in the Public Library, George's Street, Dunlaoghaire. The other Purchasing Officers are based in Cumberland House, Cumberland Street - around the corner from Westland Row. It is probable that the Dublin South Chief Purchasing Officer will be moving to Tallaght at the end of 1994, locating either in the new Library there or in the new Council offices. If you live outside Dublin, then consult your telephone directory for the address and telephone number of your own Library Service Purchasing Officer.

If you live in Northern Ireland, you should contact Mrs Anne Patterson, Central Library, Royal Avenue, Belfast, Phone (0232) 243233, who is responsible for library stocks in the Belfast area. The Western, North Eastern, South Eastern and Southern Education and Library Boards cover areas outside Belfast - consult the White Pages (under Education & Library Board) for their respective

CHAPTER 8: *Distribution*

addresses and telephone numbers. You should send your letter to the Stocks Editor of each Board.

Final piece of advice with regard to supplying the Library Service: it is no harm to follow-up your letter after a week or two with a phone call and don't be afraid to apply gentle persuasion on the phone in order to get them to take some copies; if you are not successful on the phone, seek an appointment.

CHAPTER 9

Getting the Publicity

This is the department which will require a lot of effort and hard work on your behalf - if you get no publicity for your book, you get no sales, it's as simple as that! This chapter will deal with various methods that can be employed to get as much post-launch publicity as possible for your book.

It is a good idea if you are writing a local history or a biography to appeal for information in the "Letters to the Editor" sections of all relevant newspapers during your research - this is a useful form of advance publicity. With a novel or poetry a letter to your regular newspapers stating that you are finishing your first book may also get you some worthwhile advance publicity. Check with "Books Ireland" to see when they need material for advance publicity and what details they require. Contact the Irish Writers' Centre well in advance, as they will be only too happy to advertise your book and/or launch in their own literature and Diary of Events. It is also worthwhile letting your local Arts Centre know in advance so that they can include it in their publicity material.

Where to Get It

Whenever you are seeking publicity for your book, remember one important thing: always plug where it can be bought: if you have a distributor, *underline* the fact that it is distributed by Eason's and is available in all bookshops; if you have no distributor, mention the outlets where it is available from; if you have no outlets, mention the fact that you will be in front of such-and-such a landmark every Saturday between the hours of 10am and 3pm. This is most important, as all the publicity in the world is of no value to you if people do not know where or how to purchase a copy of your work. Don't be shy - put in your plug about where your book is available.

I will now detail all the avenues that you can follow in order to secure as much publicity as possible for your book. I give it from hard experience, but remember this: do not be daunted, don't think that "it's all right for him, he is established".

CHAPTER 9: *Getting the Publicity*

Keep in mind that you have a better chance of getting publicity than an established author has, for you are a new writer, and *that* is news! It only gets difficult as you put out more books. You can capitalise on the fact that you are a new writer on the scene and you will enjoy tremendous goodwill from the media because of your novelty appeal. A first book from a new author is news, a fifth book from an established author is not news. So take your pen in your hand, be confidant and start looking for your publicity.

Book Reviews

This is one of the most important areas of your marketing campaign. You have now successfully published your book and the blaze of publicity surrounding the launch has died away. You are now depending on reviews in the books section of the various national and local newspapers in order to highlight your book and gain maximum publicity for it.

What you have to do is to send *three* copies of your book to the Editor, Arts Section, Book Reviews, (Name of major newspaper - for example the Newsletter, Belfast Telegraph, Irish News, Irish, Evening and Sunday Press, Irish and Sunday Independent and Evening Herald, Sunday Tribune, Irish Times, Cork Examiner, Evening Echo, Derry Journal), with an accompanying letter briefly outlining the content of your book and seeking a review of same. Make sure your address, telephone number and day-time phone contact are clearly stated on your letter. You might ask why three copies? If you only send one, the Editor cannot pass it on to a reviewer and glance through your book at the same time, so you need a copy for the Editor. As reviews take place not too long a spell after publication, an Editor will, in most cases, need to have two reviewers for each book supplied, in case one of them gets ill in the middle of reading your book. So the best way of guaranteeing a review is to forward three copies to the Editor.

You will also need to send three copies to the separate Books Review Editor of your local publication, be it the Dundalk Democrat, Connaught Tribune or Kerryman. Don't forget the religious media in this regard as generally such newspapers have an excellent books review feature page. Other newspapers you can contact are mentioned under the News Items heading later in this chapter.

There is no need for me to give you a detailed breakdown of the names and addresses of the various newspapers here - consult your local Golden Pages directory, under the heading "Newspapers", or in Northern Ireland the Yellow Pages under the heading "Newspapers and Magazines" for details. The Dublin 01 area Golden Pages includes many country titles under the newspapers heading. If you live or work near a city centre, you will be able to drop your books into the major newspapers in less than an hour on your bicycle. Otherwise you will have to post them, which will cost money.

Specialist Magazines

One area which many mainstream publishers overlook when seeking publicity for their publications is that of specialist magazines - Union or Staff magazines for instance. The Editors of these magazines are only too glad to receive any item of interest, particularly if it relates to their general readership. In this area you have a captive readership - whereas they may not read all of a newspaper, or just the Sports section, people do have an interest in a sectional magazine and would tend to read all of it, including your review! If you are a member, your Trade Union will be only too happy to feature your achievement in its magazine.
I have had all my books kindly reviewed in "The Review", the magazine of the Public Service Executive Union, of which I am a proud and active member.

All Unions nowadays publish professional magazines, for example INTO, the Irish National Teachers' Organisation, publish two journals, "An Múinteoir" every term and "Tuarascáil" every month and the Northern Ireland Public Service Alliance publish the excellent "NIPSA News" monthly. The magazines of some unions are published in their UK headquarters, for example "The Highway" and "The Record" are produced by the ATGWU in their London offices at Transport House, Smith Square, Westminster. Check your Golden Pages under the heading "Trade Associations & Trade Unions" and your Yellow Pages under the heading "Trade Unions" for names and telephone numbers of Unions you may wish to contact.

When I published "Dublin 7" I sent a copy to Ann Kennedy, Editor of "An Post News", the staff magazine of An Post. It got an excellent review - the connection being that the book was the first local history of a complete postal district. The An Post staff magazine is a very professional affair, with excellent lay-out and content and has a full-colour cover. Such professionalism is indicative of many specialist magazines in this day and age, so they are all well worth following up. Examples of specialist publications abound - like "Taxi", the official newspaper of the taxi trade, which can be contacted at 17, Lower Camden Street, Dublin 2.

CHAPTER 9: *Getting the Publicity*

"Dublin 7" featured the founding of the Credit Union movement, which had its roots in Dublin 7, so I got some publicity in the "Credit Union Review". I also got a mention for the book in the Annual Report of West Cabra Credit Union - I am a long-time member of that Credit Union. The "Garda Review", the magazine of the GRA, also gave the book good coverage as it featured the history of a number of Dublin 7 Garda Stations.

So look to any organisation of which you are a member, for example Trade Unions, An Oige (the Irish Youth Hostelling Association), the Credit Union, Post Office Savings Bank, AIB, Trustee Savings Bank, YHANI (Youth Hostelling Association of Northern Ireland), Cycling Club, Parish group and see if they can give your book a mention in their Newsletter, Annual Report or Broadsheet. All you have to do here is to ask anybody associated with such a group if they publish a magazine for their staff, membership or customers: for example "Irish Homes" is published for the First National Building Society and is displayed in all their branches and distributed by them to 10,000 of their mortgage holders. Most progressive clubs will have a quality newsletter, for example "Sportslink News" is the newsletter of the Public Service Telecom Sports Club in Santry, Dublin. Like many such newsletters, it is professionally and expertly produced and the newsletter of the Royal Canal Amenity Group is a classical example of the high standards of such publications.

Are there any publications covering your area of work or type of employment? For example, if you are employed in the public sector, you should contact the "Public Sector Times", which is the newspaper of the Public and Civil Service. Published monthly, it is an excellent newspaper and will certainly cover your story. You can contact the Times at 1, Eglinton Terrace, Bray, Co Wicklow, Phone (01) 286 9111. If you are employed in the public sector in Northern Ireland, each Department of Government puts out its own newsletter or magazine. Consult your White Pages for the address of the relevant (or all) Departments you wish to communicate with, sending your material to the Personnel Division.

Look for connections between your book and the myriad of organisations throughout Ireland - Licensed Vintners, grocery chains, Unions, large companies like Guinness, golf clubs, GAA clubs, soccer and rugby clubs, Tourist Information Centres, ladies clubs, even branches of unions and endeavour to get publicity in their publications. "Let your fingers do the walking..." - consult your Yellow Pages under the headings "Sports Clubs & Associations", "Institutes", "Youth & Community Groups" and "Clubs & Associations"; consult your Golden Pages under the headings "Associations & Institutes", "Social Clubs" and "Sports Clubs & Associations". Don't forget the travel companies, for example Sealink and

CHAPTER 9: *Getting the Publicity*

B&I frequently produce passenger magazines and Aer Lingus and British Midland produce in-flight magazines.

Finally, don't be snobby about seeking publicity - even a mention in the offset newsletter of a pigeon club, Union branch or youth club is good publicity!

Religious Publications

Does your church put out a parish newsletter? If so, your book may be newsworthy to them. There are many publications by all denominations including the major religious newspapers like the Baptist Times, the Catholic Herald & Standard, The Irish Catholic, The Church of England Newspaper, the Church Times and the Methodist Recorder. Catholic religious orders all have their own publications, such as the Columbans' "Far East" - the list is endless: The Reality, The Messenger, The Word - contact the Central Catholic Library, 74, Merrion Square, Dublin 2, Phone (01) 676 1264 for a complete list of Catholic publications. With regard to Church of Ireland publications, you could contact the Representative Church Body Library at Braemor Park, Dublin 14, Phone (01) 492 3979 and they will give you details of periodicals in print. Consult the phone book for details of your church, be it Society of Friends, Mormon, Methodist, Presbyterian or whatever, inquire about their publications and make your efforts. You could consider writing a story with some religious significance concerning your book, in order that it may appeal to their editorial criteria.

Alternatively, you can contact the APCK (Association for the Promotion of Christian Knowledge) Bookshops, at St Anne's Church, Dawson Street, Dublin 2, Phone (01) 661 6400 and The Cathedral, Donegal Street, Belfast, Phone (0232) 244825, for details of religious periodicals and magazines.

Finally, in regard to special interest publications, don't forget the political parties, who generally put out their own newsletters or magazines. Whatever the party, be it Fianna Fáil, Fine Gael, the SDLP, the DUP or the PD's, if your book would appeal to their interests, try and get a mention in their publications.

News Item

Some newspapers don't run a books review page, or else your book might not be suitable for a review. A useful hint here is to pick out an item in your book which may appeal to newspapers like the Star, the Sunday News, the Sunday Life or the Sunday World.

CHAPTER 9: *Getting the Publicity*

Look for an angle - for example, anybody that I know who enjoys sport gets the Star - so if there is anything on sport that could be featured as a news item in the paper, they will cover it. The Star, like the Sunday World, enjoys a huge readership, one which you cannot ignore. The Sunday World would cover your book from any interesting news angle that you can muster up - this is up to yourself and your own imagination.

The Farmers' Journal could feature your book if it contained a rural interest, so keep this important source of publicity in mind. It is very easy to overlook the rural aspect in an urban dominated lifestyle. The Sunday Business Post does not run a books page but I have found that if they can get a business line (for example a property boom in a district could be tied in with a published local history) they will run a news item on your book. Again, it is up to you to be inventive and persuasive here.

Is there any satire in your book that may appeal to the Phoenix magazine? After all, any publicity is good publicity, so don't be shy, give them a try. The Phoenix is published fortnightly by Penfield Enterprises, 44 Lower Baggot Street, Dublin 1, Phone (01) 668 2697. Its 20,000 circulation is not to be sneezed at!

If your book contains aspects of labour history you could send a copy to the Irish Labour History Society. The Society publishes a yearly diary entitled "Saothar" in addition to arranging workshops and seminars throughout the year. Contact person is Francis Devine at SIPTU headquarters, Parnell Square, Dublin 1. You can also contact the Society through their Museum at Beggars Bush Barracks, Haddington Road, Dublin 2, Phone (01) 668 1071. Finally, Ireland's Own is an excellent publication that may prove to be a suitable platform for publicising your tome.

Your Roots

Rose O Driscoll lived most of her life in Cabra West. When I published her poetry it received great publicity in Dublin, culminating in a visit by 83-year-old Rose to the Áras, where she presented a copy of her book to President Mary Robinson. I sent a copy of Rose's poetry book to the Leinster Leader, as Rose was born in Tipperkevin, Co Kildare, in 1909. They did a half-page feature on Rose and her poetry; as a result her book enjoyed keen sales in County Kildare. So if you are living in Dublin but were born elsewhere, don't forget your local newspaper back home. They are always keen for news of former residents - no matter how long it is since you departed from your roots. Go into Easons and seek out the provincial newspaper stand. Have a look at the selection and make your purchases. Look through the papers and see where you and your project fit in, then make your contact.

Your roots are very important and provincial newspapers are always keen on publicising the achievements of the sons and daughters of current or former residents of the locality. For example if your family have roots in Co Louth you could contact the Dundalk Democrat: "Daughter of Darver Carpenter Launches First Book". You can also contact Irish Clubs in areas where there is a significant concentration of emigrant Irish; you can also target emigrants from your own area, for example Malin Head emigrants in Leeds or Dubliners in Perth, Australia. You can contact the Department of Foreign Affairs, St Stephen's Green, Dublin 2, Phone (01) 4780 822 for a list of Irish Clubs world-wide. Irish Clubs publish their own magazines and exposure in them may open up a small export market for your publication, for example a feature on "North of the Liffey" in the Sydney, NSW Irish Club magazine helped to sell over 200 copies of the book through the local Irish Shop.

Local Newspapers

This area of the media world has been a growth industry in recent years. Publications such as "Local News", edited by Frank Banbrick, and "Newswest", edited by Freda Kelly, are excellent local newspapers that are always on the look-out for local developments. They will be only too happy to give you some publicity. Again, there is no need for me to give an exhaustive listing here, as there are so many of them, like the Ballymun News, The South West Express, the Fitzwilliam Post (which serves the Dublin business community) and the Limerick Observer. Consult your local phone book or Golden or Yellow Pages for details of your own district's local publications, or ask someone living in a particular locality to keep you a copy of their local paper and having read it over, make your contact.

Any Short Stories

Another way of getting publicity for your book is by writing short stories that could be geared towards the readership of a particular newspaper, then approaching the Editor with a view to letting him or her have your story free of charge, on condition that at the end of the story you are mentioned, for example:

"Joe Bloggs is an amateur historian and has recently published a book entitled 'Jamie Graham - A True World Hero'. Distributed by Easons it is available in all bookshops, price £5.95".

CHAPTER 9: *Getting the Publicity*

I have used this method on many occasions; I wrote a piece about Christmas as a child growing up in Cabra West entitled "The Cisco Kid on the 22A" and it publicised my book "Waiting for the 22". I might not have received a penny for my story, which covered a half-page in the Evening Press, but it was certainly great publicity for the book.

You may consider letting newspapers feature profiles of characters, a history of a building or quotations from poetry from your book in return for a mention. I allowed "Newswest" feature many of the characters from my book "North of the Liffey" in return for a mention in the paper. Look for the angles yourself and get to it. In any event, it all helps to build up a public image for yourself, which in turn helps sell your book.

The Book Trade

"Books Ireland" is an excellent journal and is another very useful platform in which to get some exposure for your publication in the wider book world. It is perceived as a trade magazine but has recently progressed into a general magazine for the book industry. Edited, owned and produced by Jeremy Addis at 11, Newgrove Avenue, Dublin 4, Phone (01) 269 2185, the magazine is bought by libraries and retailers worldwide, so it is a very important tool for the publisher. It may also be advisable to place a small advertisement in "Books Ireland". A quarter-page advertisement should be well within your small budget. Actually, this would probably be the only advertising necessary.

Radio

I have found Radio to be really in tune with developments on the ground and also very supportive to the arts world. With regard to RTE Radio, Donnybrook, Dublin 4, Phone (01) 208 3111, there is a host of programmes you can contact, like the Arts Show, the Sunday Show, Both Sides Now, book shows - the list is endless. Don't forget current affairs programmes - for example "Today at Five" have a books review spot. I think that the Arts Show would be your first target. If you are not a Radio lover, become one. Listen in. Find out when the programmes are on and see if your book would be of interest to the particular listenerships. A good hint here: get the RTE Guide and study the Radio section. This will give you details of all programmes and you can tune in to, get the gist of a show, see how your book would fit in and then send off a couple of copies to the producer for review.

Always keep in mind that once you appear on a Radio show, you could be shooting yourself in the foot insofar as the TV is concerned and this is something which I have learned from experience. If you appear on the Gaybo Hour or the Pat Kenny Show on RTE Radio, you may never get on to any TV show, such is the extreme rivalry between the two services. But a *guarantee* of an appearance on Radio is a thousand times better than a remote possibility that you may get a stint on TV - and in this day of video and TV entertainment, don't <u>ever</u> underestimate the power of the Radio! I got on the Andy O Mahony Sunday Programme on RTE and anyone I bumped into for months after that would greet me with the words "I heard you on the Andy O Mahony Show". Two weeks after that Radio appearance "Dublin Seven" entered the bestsellers list at Number 6. A review on Gaybo's RTE Radio show in February 1984 helped sell out the first print run of my book "A History of Cabra and Phibsborough".

So remember - don't waste your time and hard effort, go on the Radio when you get the chance, get your publicity and sell your books. This advice is all from my own experience and from talking to many fringe writers and publishers in the art world.

An appearance on Radio will help shift your books off the shelf, and if that happens, some shops will start to promote your book themselves; if you then get into the bestsellers list, that in itself is publicity and will help sell even more books. If you by-pass Radio and are unsuccessful trying to get onto the TV, your book will shortly become yesterday's news and in the end you won't even get on the Radio. So go straight for the Radio at the very beginning. If your Radio appearance results in you having a best-seller on your hands, the TV producers may well be knocking on *your* door, saving you the bother of having to chase them! Finally, can you speak Irish? If so, contact Radio na Gaeltachta on the same telephone number as RTE and try and get on air as Gaeilge.

If you live in Northern Ireland, you should try BBC Radio Ulster or Radio Foyle - they are based at 8, Northland Road, Derry, Phone (0504) 262244. For Radio stations in the province you can consult your Yellow Pages under the heading "Broadcasting Services" or alternatively contact the Radio Authority, 70, Brompton Road, London SW3 1EY, Phone (071) 430 2724. They will provide you with an up-to-date list of all Radio stations operating in Northern Ireland. Remember that Radio programming is varied, and that you have a good chance of getting exposure on most current affairs shows. Consult your TV Times for details on the various Radio programmes, listen in to particular shows, then send in your book for a review. It would be no harm to set out in your letter where you think your book could slot into the format of a particular show.

CHAPTER 9: *Getting the Publicity*

Local Radio

When I mention Radio I include all forms of Radio, including Local Radio. From Tralee to Drogheda, Dundalk to Sligo, Bray to Wexford, Local Radio is now a huge industry and I know of very many people from ages twenty to eighty who prefer Local Radio to TV viewing. Stations like Dublin's Anna Livia are very supportive to the arts and to local communities, so go on, get on your local station. However, one little piece of advice here: do try and get on RTE Radio, BBC Radio or Radio na Gaeltachta before your local debut!

If you live in the Dublin area, Radio Anna Livia FM transmits on 103.8 FM and is on the air from 5pm to midnight Monday to Fridays and from 9am to midnight at weekends. It is based at 3, Grafton Street, Dublin 1, Phone (01) 677 8103. For your own local Radio Station, contact your phone book or the Golden Pages under the heading of "Radio Stations". Alternatively, you can contact the Irish Radio and Television Commission, Marine Terrace, Clanwilliam Court, Dublin 2, Phone (01) 676 0966, for a complete up-to-date list of all Radio stations operating in the State. They will post or fax you the list on request.

By the way, do not overlook another important Radio medium, and that is hospital Radio. I have given interviews on the Mater Hospital Radio on a number of occasions. It is an important platform for you and the audience is not insignificant - get in touch with your local hospital and find out who to contact. Then get on the hospital airwaves and enjoy yourself!

Notice how I always spell Radio with a capital R - that is because I am aware of the tremendous importance of the medium and the fact that hundreds of thousands of people listen to various stations every day - a key market source for your book.

While I am on the subject of the Radio, I have to mention Gay Byrne, who is part and parcel of contemporary Irish life. He has, over the years, been one of the most supportive people in this country to up-and-coming and emerging artists; he will always give the unrecognised a plug if at all possible and is most encouraging to unknown artists. Simply write to him care of RTE Radio, Donnybrook, Dublin 4, setting out truthfully your status, your work, how you came to write and publish your book and your personal circumstances. If at all possible, he will feature your work on his programme.

Finally, a novel way of getting publicity on all-music Radio stations is to think up some questions for a telephone quiz based on your book, then contact the chosen station with a view to them running a telephone quiz. Signed copies of your work

52

can be given out by a presenter to all telephone callers with the correct answers. It's a great way of getting added publicity for your book. I have also successfully used this angle to get publicity in newspapers long after the media coverage of a particular book has dried up!

Don't be Nervous

Final piece of advice with regard to Radio: if you are lucky to get on any of the shows, relax! I have even given interviews on Radio na Gaeltactha where I would be a little nervous with my Cabra West Irish, but I was given plenty of time and encouragement and the interviews went off well! Andy O Mahony eased me into his programme and ensured that I was not swamped by the participative nature of his show and Mike Murphy casually brought me, a very nervous rookie, through the rigours of my very first radio interview on the Arts Show. Radio presenters are highly professional and know how to make you relax, so don't worry about being nervous and good luck on the airwaves!

TV

By its very nature, television is a difficult medium for you to gain exposure for your work, so don't put all your energy on TV publicity and do your best to get on Radio. Also, you should keep in mind the fact that TV may be a bit ambitious on your first book, even though from my own experience I have found TV presenters to be very supportive - I bumped into Frank Hall in the grounds of RTE following a Radio interview that I gave about my book "Irish Lives". After a brief chat, I presented him with a copy of "Confessions of a Court Clerk", which I had published at the same time as "Irish Lives". "I'll see what I can do", he said to me. A couple of months later I saw an article about the book in "Ireland's Own" - written by Frank Hall. Thanks Frank!

RTE TV

With regard to RTE Television, it looks like it will not have a books programme like "Books 94" and "Booklines" for the 1994/95 season. For the novice, "Booklines" presented a programme on local history in mid-January and also around the same time did a piece on small publishers. If any replacement is recorded for these shows in the future (watch the RTE Guide) it is advisable to get your book to the producer in plenty of time so as to be included in the order of programming, for a lot of research is done in the four to six weeks leading up to a particular show. Indeed, you should send your book in as soon as it is published.

CHAPTER 9: *Getting the Publicity*

There are numerous RTE TV programmes which you can try, including "Live at Three" and News Features. Check the RTE Guide and see where your book slots in. Don't forget "Cúrsaí" on RTE2, which gives exposure to new and emerging talent - if you or your book has any connection to the Irish language, send a copy into them and follow-up immediately with a telephone call to the producer.

Liam O Murchú is a presenter with a great eye for the grassroots of Irish society - north or south - he did an excellent "Trom agus Eadtrom" programme on RTE which featured boxing legends and centred on the late Garda, Jim "Lugs" Branigan. The airing of the programme coincided with the launch of my biography on Jim entitled "Lugs", which helped it into the bestsellers' list. His "Lifelines" programme during the summer of 1994 was very supportive of local initiative throughout Ireland.

You can contact the various TV personalities and producers by writing to RTE, Donnybrook, Dublin 4, Phone (01) 208 3111 and RTE, Farnham House, Great Victoria Street, Belfast, Phone (0232) 326441.

Northern Ireland TV

Programmes on Northern Ireland TV which you can try include "Morning Extra", which goes out every morning from Monday to Friday and "Good Morning Ulster", which is broadcast every morning from 7 until 8.45 am. In each case send your book into the Producer of the particular programme, BBC Northern Ireland, 25, Ormeau Avenue, Belfast 2, Phone (0232) 338000. The "Gerry Anderson Show" may also be interested in featuring your story and this is shown on Friday evenings. Write to Charlie Warmington enclosing a copy of your book and setting out your background and reason for publishing your work. In each case follow-up your letter with a phone-call after about a week.

With regard to Ulster TV, Havelock House, Ormeau Road, Belfast, Phone (0232) 241080/328122, "Live at Six" has an excellent features content and they may be interested in featuring your work. Write to Jimie De Largy, Features, Live at Six, enclosing a copy of your book. "Kelly" is another programme that you might have success with, particularly as they are trying to get more and more local people featured. A one-and-a-half hour show which is broadcast every Friday night, it is produced by Philip Kampff. Send your book into Philip with a brief covering letter. You may also wish to try British Sky Broadcasting, 6 Centaurs Business Park, Grant Way, Isleworth, London, Phone (071) 782 3000.

Practical advice regarding any TV programme: about a fortnight after you have sent in your book, follow-up with a phone call to the producer. Find out if your

54

CHAPTER 9: *Getting the Publicity*

book is being featured. If they are lukewarm about it, send in another letter and highlight all the positive, interesting and newsworthy items concerning your book - and good luck. Finally, if you think your book has broader appeal beyond the shores of Ireland, why not try BBC and the independent TV network in the UK. Consult the TV Times for programming. Good luck on TV.

Book Signing

This is another way of securing publicity for your book. Approach the main stores and see if their book buyers will arrange a signing. Try and arrange this in conjunction with a newspaper interview or a radio appearance. Tell the book-buyer that you are doing an interview and could mention the fact that you will be doing a book signing in their shop next Saturday morning. If you are successful, send out a press release, giving details and times of your book signing. Don't be choosey in this regard. If you can arrange a book signing in the Roselawn Bookstore, Castleknock, it could secure you a write-up in "Newswest", thus giving you exposure in Dublin West. Likewise a book signing in Easons in the Town Centre could result in a write-up in "Local News", thus giving you exposure in the greater Tallaght area.

If you cannot arrange for a bookshop to allow you have a signing, how about a hotel, café or pub? I couldn't get any bookshops in Perth to allow me perform a signing of "Irish Lives", so I approached the Langley Hotel and persuaded the management there to allow me arrange a signing in their "Fenian's Bar". I sold over 250 books during an afternoon signing and was subsequently approached by Angus & Robertson (the Easons of Perth) to sign books in three of their bookstores. A major plus in doing a book-signing in a hotel or pub is that 100% of the retail price of the book goes into your own pocket!

Spot Prizes

I have found that offering copies of my books to a range of people and groups as spot prizes is a great way of highlighting my work. It could be your factory's Christmas Party, an office night out at the bowling alley or a pub quiz. A raffle at a school's annual dance or your Union Conference's dinner, the All Priests' Show or a Trocaire fundraiser. Whatever it is, offer signed copies, free of charge, to the organiser. The publicity is worth it and your book is being talked about during the night and for long afterwards. It is as effective a method of publicity as a write-up in the paper. In addition, it does help you to build up a public profile, be it in your own suburb, town or even city! Be generous in this regard - give and you will reap the harvest.

CHAPTER 9: *Getting the Publicity*

Going for a Reprint?

Don't forget, a reprint of a book is news, so draw up a suitable press release - KISS, don't go over a page - giving details of original print run, how quickly it sold out and number of copies being reprinted. Send this press release to all newspapers, periodicals, radio stations and TV. Go over the same ground that you covered on the original edition and send them your catchy press release. It would be no harm to send a covering letter with your press release to all those publications which gave your book a write-up, thanking them for the coverage, "which no doubt greatly helped to sell out the first edition", and asking them to give the occasion of the reprint a mention.

Local Talks

I have given talks on local history around Dublin, in community centres, libraries and even in the Dominican Priory in Tallaght. I brought copies of my local history books with me and in every case sold around a dozen copies - better than having them lying in the attic! I gave talks in libraries in Western Australia on the history of the Irish in that State. On one occasion I sold fifty copies of "Irish Lives" after presenting a talk in Albany, in the south west of the State. So look to this avenue too as a medium for selling and publicising your work.

Non-Print Artistic Work

If you are a keen musician or talented singer, the advice given in this chapter, along with the information given regarding a public Launch and supplying the Library Service, can also relate to the publication of an audio-cassette tape or a compact disc (for example the Library Service may be interested in purchasing your work for their music-lending departments - I bet you forgot that!). If you are recording music or song, you can take all the steps which I have set out in this book to assist you along the way. Good luck!

Irish Language Media

It is always worthwhile to prepare an Irish-language version of your press release. Note such papers as "ANOIS" and "LÁ" - don't forget them when you are sending out photos, book jackets and the like. Radio na Life is a lively Dublin radio station and a new television channel, Telefís na Gaeilge, is on its way. Even the professional publishers are often sadly remiss in this respect.

CAIBIDIL 10

An Leabhar Gaeilge É?

B'fhéidir gur scríobh tú do leabhar as Gaeilge. Más mar sin é, caithfidh tú na rudaí seo a leanas a dhéanamh:

An Réamhrá: Caithfidh tú d'intinn a dhéanamh suas cén duine ba mhaith leat chun réamhrá a scríobh. Más leabhar spóirt é, cosúil le leabhar ar an iomáint nó ar an bpeil, b'fhéidir go mba mhaith leat duine cosúil le Cathaoirleach Chumann Lúthchleas Gael nó Micheál Ó Muircheartaigh lena scríobh duit. Má tá urscéal, leabhar ceoil nó staire agat, b'fhéidir go mba mhaith leat duine ó Chonradh na Gaeilge nó Gael Linn chun an réamhrá a scríobh.

An Raidió: Is é an chéad rud le déanamh ná glaoch ar Raidió na Gaeltachta agus labhairt leo mar gheall ar do leabhar. Déan socrú bheith ar an raidió lá na láinseála féin nó lá arna mharach. Déan iarracht freisin scéal a fháil ar an Nuacht mar gheall ar an láinseáil. Mar sin gheobhaidh tú "dhá ghreim den silín". Is féidir leat do leabhar a chur go dtí na clárreachtairí éagsúla i Raidió na Gaeltachta - glaoigh ar an stáisiún chun na hainmneacha go léir a fháil. Tá oifig ag an stáisiún i gContae na Gaillimhe agus oifig eile in mBaile Átha Cliath - in RTÉ, Domhnach Broc, BÁC 4, Guthán (01) 208 3111 - bain trial freisin ar RTE féin!

Téann Raidió na Life amach ar 102 FM, stáisiún iontach a chraolann as Baile Átha Cliath le haghaidh 150,000 daoine nó mar sin a labhrann Gaeilge i timpeallacht na cathrach. Ritheann Comharchumann Raidió Átha Cliath an stáisiún. Faoi láthair, tá an stáisiún ar an aer ó 5pm go dtí 10.30pm gach oíche agus ó 11am go dtí 1pm gach deireadh seachtain. Tá oifig Radió na Life suite in uimhir 7, Cearnóg Mhuirfeann, Baile Átha Cliath 2, Guthán (01) 661 6333.

Cuireann Raidió Foyle cláracha Gaeilge amach agus b'fhéidir go mbeadh suim acu i do leabhar. Tá oifig an stáisiúin sin suite i nDoire Cholmcille, ag uimhir 8, Sráid Northland, Guthán (0504) 262244. Is cuid de BBC Raidió Uladh é Raidió Foyle. Is féidir leat scríobh chuig an BBC freisin - tá a oifig suite i mBéal Feirste, ag uimhir 25, Ascaill Ormeau, Guthán (0232) 338000.

CAIBIDIL 10: *An Leabhar Gaeilge É?*

Na Nuachtáin: An nuachtán is tábhachtaí, measaim, ná "ANOIS", agus tagann sé amach gach seachtain, maidin Dé Sathairn. Déan an-iarracht scéal a fháil sa nuachtán sin mar gheall ar an láinseáil. Is féidir leat dul ar ais arís go dtí an tEagarthóir chun cuntas a fháil le haghaidh clúdach an leabhair - agus is féidir leat iarraidh ar Bernard Harris, Eagarthóir ANOIS, critique a chur ar fáil. Arís, bí macánta anseo - faigh ANOIS, léigh é agus faigh amach cén chuid den nuachtán a d'oirfeadh do do leabhar. Is féidir leat ANOIS a fháil trí do shiopa nuachtán féin. Tá oifig ANOIS suite in uimhir 27, Cearnóg Mhuirfean, Baile Átha Cliath 2, Guthán (01) 676 0268.

Tagann an nuachtán "SAOL" amach gach dhá mhí. Foilsítear é ó 7, Cearnóg Mhuirfean, oifig Bhord na Gaeilge. Nuachtán saor in aisce é seo. Foilsítear an nuachtán "LÁ" i mBéal Feirste agus tagann sé amach gach Déardaoin - scríobh chuig an tEagarthóir, Cúltúrlann Mac Adam Ó Fiaich, 216 Bóthar na bhFál, BT 12 6AH, Guthán (0232) 239303. Tagann "COMHAR" amach gach mí; iris atá ann a fhoilsítear ag 5, Ré Muirfean, BÁC 2. Tá iris freisin ag Conradh na Gaeilge, 6, Sráid Fhearchair, BAC 2, Guthán (01) 475 7401; tagann "FEASTA" amach gach mhí - is féidir leat scríobh chuig an tEagarthóir, Feasta, 13 Paráid na Díge, Corcaigh. Tagann iris darb ainm "Fortnight" amach i mBéal Feirste agus bíonn an-suim acu i gcúrsaí Gaeilge. Tagann "AGUS" amach gach mhí - scríobh chuig AGUS Teoranta, Gleann Maghair, Corcaigh, Guthán (021) 821116.

Tagann irisí éagsúla amach ar fud na tíre - cosúil le "AN DRÉIMIRE" (do lucht Ardteiste, míosúil ó Mhean Fomhair go dtí Aibreán, Guthán (01) 676 7283; "AN tULTACH", (míosachán, Guthán (0232) 612707; "AN TIMIRE", (iris ráithiúil, Guthán (01) 872 9935; "AN SAGART", (iris ráithiúil, Guthán (01) 682 5222 agus "MAHOGANY GASPIPE", (gach trí mhí, iris ráithiúil le haghaidh mhargadh déagóirí, Guthán (01) 676 3222). Is féidir leat eolas a fháil faoi na hirisí seo ó Bord na Gaeilge, 7, Cearnóg Muirfean, BÁC 2, Guthán (01) 676 3222. Is féidir leat freisin do leabhar a chuir isteach chuig Bord na Gaeilge chun píosa a fháil i "AN LÉITHEOIR", iris shuimiúil a thugann eolas ar leabhair nua sa mhargadh i nGaeilge agus i mBéarla.

Ar fhreastail tú ar scoil lán-Gaeilge? Má fhreastail, bíonn nuachtlitir á cur amach acu go minic, agus b'fhéidir go mbeidh tú ábalta scéal a fháil i nuachtlitir do sheanscoile féin. Freisin, tá iris an-mhaith le haghaidh na nGaelscoileanna go léir faoin teideal "Gaelscoileanna". Tagann an iris seo amach gach téarma, ceithre huaire sa bhliain. Bain triail as - scríobh chuig an Eagarthóir, Vivian Uíbh Eachach, "Gaelscoileanna", 7 Cearnóg Muirfean, Baile Átha Cliath 2, Guthán (01) 676 3222 - agus déan do dhícheall píosa a fháil san iris seo. Tagann "An tEolaí", Nuachtlitir Eolaíochta na nIar-Bhunscoileanna, gach mhí.

Le críochnú, ná déan dearmad ar na hirisí éagsúla, mar shampla na hirisí atá ag na ceardchumainn agus dreamanna cosúil le Gardaí, múinteoirí agus dochtúirí - tá dhá iris an-mhaith ag an INTO, "An Múinteoir" (gach tearma) agus "Tuarascáil" (gach mí).

Agus ná dearmad ar na nuachtán Bhéarla, mar go minic bíonn colún Gaeilge acu, cosúil leis an "Irish Times", Sráid Dólier, Baile Átha Cliath 2, Guthán (01) 679 2022 agus 110, Sráid Mhór Victoria, Béal Feirste 2, Guthán (0232) 323324, atá go han-mhaith don teanga náisiúnta.

An Teilifís: Bain triail as an gclár "Cúrsaí" a bhíonn ar siúl gach oíche Luan, Máirt, Deardaoin agus Aoine, ar RTE2 ag a leath-huair taréis a hocht agus an gclár "Cúrsaí Ealaíne", ar an stáisiún céanna oíche Dé Domhnaigh. Is féidir leat glaoch ar an gclárreachtaire in RTÉ, Domhnach Broc, BÁC 4, Guthán (01) 208 3111.

Dáiliúchán: Bain triail as ÁIS, Áisinteacht Dáiliúchán Leabhar, 31, Sráid na bhFiníní, Baile Átha Cliath 2, Guthán (01) 661 6522, nó as Eason's (féach ar Caibidil 8). Má theipeann ort dáilitheoir a fháil, caithfidh tú gabháil thart timpeall na siopaí-leabhar éagsúla chun do shaothar a dhíol. Chun do leabhar a dhíol ag imeachtaí Gaelacha ar fud na tíre, is féidir leat eolas a fháil mar gheall ar na haontaí, fleánna agus feiseanna éagsúla ó Chomhdháil Náisiúnta na Gaeilge, 46 Sráid Chill Dara, BÁC 2, Guthán (01) 679 4780.

TRÓCAIRE

HELPING PEOPLE TO HELP THEMSELVES

For the past 21 years you've helped Trócaire support thousands of people in Africa, Asia, and Latin America in their struggle for development, equality and justice.

Trócaire supports hundreds of long-term development projects to help poor communities help themselves; improving healthcare facilities, providing basic skills and training and working for human rights.

But there are still millions who need your long term support. Please give generously to Trócaire, because what you give today will bring hope to the people of the developing world for years to come.

Send anything you can to:

TRÓCAIRE
The Catholic Agency for World Development

169 Booterstown Avenue, Blackrock, Co Dublin. (01) 288 5385.
12 Cathedral Street, Dublin 1. Telephone: (01) 874 3875.
50 King Street, Belfast BT1 6AD. Telephone (0232) 238586.
9 Cook Street, Cork. Telephone: (021) 275622.

Chapter 11

One Year Later

Time passes by and it is now the first anniversary of the publication of your book. If it was a modest success and went to a second print, the chances are that your have not sold your entire second print, nor are you now likely to sell it out, as the prominent shelf-display life of your book has by this time expired. Your distributor now wants you to collect all remainders and finally settle your account.

What are you to do with the two or three, or even four hundred copies that are left over? Give them out as presents? Here is my advice: if the book enjoyed a modest success, it will still be remembered in the book trade. In my case, I approached Alan Hosgood, manager of Eason's Bargain Basement, in their O Connell Street branch. He agreed to take my remainders at a unit cost of between 80p to 115p per book - which might be below cost but beats having dust accumulating on packages of books which will only lose value as time goes by. Depending on the track record of your book, you will be able to negotiate a mutually agreeable price with Eason's Bargain Books section.

Nowadays, most bookshops will have bargain sections and you can try them too. (I tried to sell my hardback copies of "Confessions of a Court Clerk" to Chapters in Abbey Street - I didn't get past the front desk, much to the surprise of the cashier then on duty. Easons took a supply and sold it out!). Second-hand bookshops are also a good source for disposing of remainders, though you will not get as good a return here as with Eason's or other bookshops.

Creative Work To Let

If your book was a novel, you may think of approaching one of the radio stations to see if they would be interested in serialising it on a particular programme. If you are successful your leftovers could be mopped up and who knows, you may even consider a reprint! Likewise, you could try and get the newspapers, either

Chapter 11: *One Year Later*

a national or a local one, to serialise your book - nothing ventured, nothing gained.

Have you ever seen posters featuring poetry or anecdotes on the London Underground or the Dublin DART? With any creative work, including poetry and even local history, you could approach the DART authorities (Dublin Area Rapid Transport), Northern Ireland Railways, Iarnród Éireann, CIE or Dublin Bus, with a view to getting boards or posters produced of extracts of your material for display in their rail and bus coaches. Likewise any hotelier, restaurant or pub could be approached to display your material if it is in a presentable package - it boils down to yourself in the end. Look for opportunities, approach the relevant people with your ideas and good luck!

If you are canvassing with a view to getting your work publicly displayed, it is worth remembering that extracts with apt illustrations would be far more attractive for display purposes than just printed material.

Novel Effort

I thought of a novel way of disposing of my remainders a few years ago. If you have a lot of books left and cannot get Easons Bargain Basement to take many off your hands, you should consider approaching some local business or factory that your book has some relevance to. Suggest to the Personnel Manager that they might consider giving each member of their staff a copy of your book as a Christmas gift - with the added carrot that you will personally sign each copy of the book. The most you could hope to ask for per book is around the £1 to £1.50 mark - not a bad price as it is money in your pocket and a novel way of getting rid of your remainders. (However, if the staff in the firm normally get a bottle of whisky for Christmas and get your signed book instead - avoid the workers for at least six months!).

If you are working on another project, this effort can be a way of getting funds for your next publication. I got a company to take two hundred copies of "North of the Liffey - A Character Sketchbook" at £1.20 per copy, on condition that I signed each one and in addition mentioned the company as a sponsor in my next book "Lugs". The Marketing Manager of the company insisted on being mentioned in "Lugs" as part of the deal. I had about 300 copies of "North of the Liffey" left over and needed funds to clear off my debt on that publication before proceeding to publish "Lugs". We shook hands on the deal and I got a cheque for £240, thus getting rid of most of my remainders and clearing off my printer's bill in full. So explore this avenue - be inventive, pushy and positive!

Another idea for disposing of your leftovers would be to approach a rugby or football club with a view to getting them to buy four, five or six hundred of your books and using them as inserts in their match programmes. You would have to sell your books at less than £1 each in order to make this proposition attractive. You could also approach a club or your Credit Union with a view to them buying a large batch of your books for insertion in an annual report or other publication. Approach promoters of concerts in Dalymount, the Dublin Horse Show, Listowel Races, Wexford Opera Festival, the Holiday Fair, in fact any event, if you feel that your book would be ideal for insertion in their programmes.

Finally, with your last few copies, you can do the rounds of second-hand bookshops and sell them off for whatever you can get. Alternatively, you can store them away in your attic for ten or twenty years, by which time it may have become a collectors item. You can then ask your price per copy - you're in the money!!

Total Commercial Failure?

Was your book a total, or almost a total failure? Did you get 2,000 printed and only sold 200? What you should do in this event is discuss you book with a few knowledgeable people and get their ideas on it. Maybe the timing was wrong - I expected to sell at least 5,000 copies of "Dublin 7". Shortly after launching it the currency crisis broke out. At £5.95, over the Christmas period bookshops could get IR£6.60 for an equivalent book published in England, due to the exchange rate fluctuations. As a result my book found it almost impossible to get adequate shelf space. When it did get shelf space following devaluation of the Irish pound, I had exhausted all my publicity. I still have 700 copies from an initial print run of 3,000 on my hands, nearly two years later! So timing can often go haywire, no matter how well you plan out your project.

If you had a really good book you could consider a new cover and a re-launch. You could get a company or business to sponsor the new cover. Maybe it was the title or possibly the photograph on the front cover that contributed to the low volume of sales? You can re-title the book or change the cover photograph. In any event a re-covering job may work and help you off-load all your books. Nothing ventured, nothing gained! Futureprint or your local printer will re-cover your book at a reasonable cost.

Chapter 11: *One Year Later*

Writers' Groups

Once published, you might consider joining some writing organisations, such as the Irish Writers Union or PEN. The Irish Writers' Union/Comhar na Scríbhneoirí is located at 19, Parnell Square, Dublin 1 and the Annual Membership is £20. If you are as yet unpublished they have an Associate Membership available at a reduced cost. Before the IWU was formed, publishing contracts were rare and payment of royalties rarer still. The Union was a prime mover in initiating and securing funds for the Irish Writers Centre at Parnell Square, next door to and linked to the Dublin Writers' Museum.

PEN is an international writers' organisation with over 10,000 members in eighty countries. The Irish Centre, PEN, was established in 1921 with Lady Gregory as its first President. Meetings are held on the second Thursday of each month in the United Arts Club, 3, Upper Fitzwilliam Street, Dublin 2. PEN can be contacted through Arthur Flynn, their Secretary, Phone (01) 668 3571. Current fees are £15 a year for full membership and £8 a year for associate membership. You may also wish to join one of the many writers' groups scattered throughout the country. There are writers' groups in existence from Sligo to Ramelton, Finuge to Inisbofin Island and Tallaght to Mountjoy Prison. For a detailed list contact the Irish Writers' Centre.

As a publisher you may consider joining CLÉ, the Irish Book Publishers' Association. Founded in 1970, it has been an important player in the growth and development of the Irish publishing industry during the 1970's and 1980's. CLÉ is located at 19, Parnell Square, Dublin 1, Phone (01) 872 9090 and Hillary Kennedy is the Administrator. Membership costs £130 a year, though the Association are bringing in a special, subsidised membership rate for emerging publishers.

Finally, please keep in mind that your first book, however published, is only just the beginning of your CV. Happy writing!

CHAPTER 12

And Finally

Congratulations are in order following the successful publication of your own book. All copies have now been disposed of and by now you are, hopefully, looking to your next book. Having done all your sums, you have probably more or less broken even. Any profits you may have made are probably in the three figure bracket, though you just might make a four figure nest egg, for example £10.99. Just remember, if there were big punts in it, you would not be publishing the manuscript yourself.

If, and it is a big IF, there are big punts in it and your book enjoyed great success with your first and second prints running out in a matter of one or two months, go directly to a big publisher and negotiate purchase of publishing rights on mutual terms. A one-man-band is alright for a small success, but if it is getting out of hand, go to a big publisher and hand over the job. With your book enjoying such great success you will be in a much stronger bargaining position than if you were only starting out trying to get it published. You could negotiate your own terms and with the manuscript being camera-ready, the big publisher could have ten or twenty thousand copies out in a matter of a week and have it distributed world-wide, a task that may be beyond the resources of most self-publishers.

As I said in the beginning of the book, you can try "The CLÉ Directory of the Irish Book World", the "Writers' and Artists Yearbook", "Books Ireland" and the weekly British book trade magazine "The Bookseller" for complete details on possible publishers in your chosen subject.

Charities

The only advice I wish to give in this chapter is the following: remember our lesser well-off brethren. In any book that I have published since "Confessions of a Court Clerk" I have always included some free advertisements for Third World organisations such as Trócaire or Goal. There are countless organisations working for the development of countries which have been devastated by First

CHAPTER 12: *And Finally*

World greed and bottomless economic requirements. You can help these organisations in your own small way by including a couple of free advertisements in your publication.

Organisations would be only too happy to provide you with camera-ready copy and would design an advertisement to tailor the content or format of your proposed book. So go on, give them a platform to reach your readership. Choose your organisation, be it your local Hospice, the Society of St Vincent de Paul or Respect. With regard to the Third World the organisations are many and varied: APSO, Concern, Goal, Gorta, Oxfam, UNESCO, UNHCR, Skillshare Africa, Trocaire or Viatores Christi. There are many others and if you wish you can contact APSO, the Agency for Personal Service Overseas, 29, Fitzwilliam Square, Dublin 2, Phone (01) 661 4411 for a detailed list or consult your phone book.

If you have made a few pounds at the end of the day, well done! If the book is readily identifiable as in the creative category, like a novel, short stories, poetry or drama, you need not pay a penny tax on your literary earnings. You can contact the Revenue Commissioners or a friendly tax adviser for details. Consult your phone book for telephone numbers. However, from experience I know that the self-publisher need not even think about the Man From Revenue (unless you become an overnight, runaway maga-success story), so....... happy self-publishing and good luck!

Notes

Notes

Notes

Notes

Notes

Notes